An Unsentimental Education

Edited by Molly McQuade **An Unsentimental Education**

Writers and Chicago

The University of Chicago Press
Chicago & London

Molly McQuade is a consultant to the New York State Council on the Arts and a contributing editor for *Booklist*.

The University of Chicago Press, Chicago 60637
The University of Chicago Press, Ltd., London
© 1995 by The University of Chicago
All rights reserved. Published 1995
Printed in the United States of America
04 03 02 01 00 99 98 97 96 95   1 2 3 4 5
ISBN: 0-226-56210-7 (cloth)

Library of Congress Cataloging-in-Publucation Data

An unsentimental education : writers and Chicago / edited by Molly McQuade.
          p.   cm.
      Includes index.
      1. American literature—Illinois—Chicago—History and criticism—Theory, etc.   2. American literature—20th century—History and criticism—Theory, etc.   3. Chicago (Ill.)—Intellectual life—20th century.   4. Authors, American—Illinois—Chicago—Interviews.   5. Authors, American—20th century—Interviews.   6. Chicago (Ill.)—In literature.   I. Title.
      PS285.C47M38   1995
      810.9′977311′0904—dc20   94-43441
                                                                             CIP

The paper used in this publication meets the minimum requirements of the American National Standard for Information Sciences—Permanence of Paper for Printed Library Materials, ANSI Z39.48-1984.

"Just a Lively Boy" was previously published in George J. Searles, ed., *Conversations with Philip Roth* (Jackson: University Press of Mississippi, 1992). © 1992 by Molly McQuade.
"Janet Lewis and the Poetry Club" was previously published in Richard Stern, *One Person and Another: On Writers and Writing* (Dallas: Baskerville Publishers, 1993). Reprinted by permission.

Contents

Acknowledgments

The University of Chicago Writer's Project and this book were funded by the Blum-Kovler Foundation. Marjorie Kovler lived in the Hyde Park section of Chicago much of her life. Both of her sons went to the University of Chicago Laboratory School and the youngest, Peter, graduated from the university. Marjorie was an enthusiast for what she believed were the university's higher interests, and her sons have, in different ways, realized those interests in their lives. She felt deeply the tragic waste and despair of the inner city. It is no accident that her oldest son, Jonathan, taught for a while in an inner city school and that Peter once worked for a black newspaper. The foundation which embodies those interests rewards teachers in such schools and does much to further the creative bonds between the communities of despair and prosperity. (It may be said that one of the strongest of those bonds is the city's famous basketball team, whose most gifted player, perhaps the most famous athlete in the world, Michael Jordan, was recruited by Jonathan when he was the team's managing partner.) This is a note of memory and gratitude from the University of Chicago to Marjorie, her husband Everett, her sons, and their foundation.

Introduction

Writers are both born and made, and their teachers share in the making of them. But in what way?

That was one of the questions being asked at the time of the University of Chicago's centennial. Chicago, like most universities, has long welcomed students who are writers, and has taken pride in others who have eventually become writers, but apparently no one had looked directly or in detail at this habit, this relation. Was an academic education useful to the writers? Were thorns concealed in it? Years later, what did the writers remember of Chicago? What mattered to them about it? How had the university passed into the life of their writing, if it had?

To find out, I was invited by the university to interview novelists and poets who had been associated, in one way or another, with Chicago in its first century. There were a great many of them. Of those who could be located, not all were available to us. I interviewed those I could, taping our conversations. Once transcribed, each interview was edited to read as a monologue in the voice of the writer. Unless they chose not to, the writers read my edited version and were free to suggest changes. Two interviews were conducted by others: Saul Bellow by Janis Bellow, and Janet Lewis by Richard Stern (who had initiated the project). The interviews with Robert Coover and Saul Bellow are in the form they preferred, questions and answers.

It may seem unusual to ask writers to talk rather than write about themselves and their education. Yet we assumed that the monologues would preserve a tone of voice or mind—a sense of the speaker—that could be interesting in its own terms.

In Philip Roth's case, the university "allowed for a nice amalgamation of the raucous and the serious. Superego Fights Id to Fifteen-Round Draw; Blood Drawn." Roth received an M.A. in English from Chicago in 1955, returned to the university to teach English from 1956 to 1958, and wrote, while at Chicago, most of the stories published in his first book, *Goodbye, Columbus.*

That book was later edited by the poet George Starbuck while he was working at Houghton Mifflin; Starbuck had once been a fellow student of Roth's. Of his own experience at Chicago, Starbuck says, "I wouldn't hold Chicago up as a Platonic model of what the academy for young writers ought to be. But what happened there was good." He learned how to read closely, "while being a snotty youth and finding ways of differing loudly with my teachers."

Some writers were influenced profoundly by particular professors. Robert Coover dedicated his first novel, *The Origin of the Brunists,* to Richard McKeon for McKeon's "revelatory impact" and "demanding standards." Recalls Coover, "I wanted to be provoked and tested. I got my wish." In the first meeting of Coover's first class with him, McKeon asked, "Mr. Coover, what does Spinoza have to say about God?" Coover collected himself. "About God? I couldn't remember a single mention of God in the entire text. The only thing I felt was that I'd just been fingered by Him."

Leon Forrest, searching for a way to create something from the "chaos" of "all of this life bubbling around," found an "intellectual father" in Allison Davis and an "intellectual uncle" in Perrin Lowrey. Douglas Unger found something similar in Richard Stern. For George Steiner, Allen Tate helped fill the role. Hayden Carruth met up with several who shared it: Paul Goodman, Norman Maclean, J. V. Cunningham, Napier Wilt.

Susan Sontag, who switched to Chicago from Berkeley as an unusually young and precocious undergraduate, was "taught incredible reading skills" there, but she discovered that she "had no creative powers at all" while a citizen in the university's "benevolent dictatorship." And she harbored no regrets about that. Sontag thrived on her classes with Joseph Schwab, "the best embodiment of Chicago's version of the Socratic method," and enjoyed others with Kenneth Burke, Edward Rosenheim, Richard McKeon, and Leo Strauss—and with Philip Rieff, whom she married two weeks after starting to audit his Social Science II course.

The people they met were part of what they learned, whether at school or in the city beyond.

The Yugoslav-born poet Charles Simic, who studied at the university by night and worked at the *Chicago Sun-Times* during the day, was told by Nelson Algren at a party, "What do you want to read [Robert Lowell] for? A kid like you, just off the boat? Read Whitman, read Sandburg, read Vachel Lindsay." Simic took him up on it.

Marguerite Young, a graduate student of R. S. Crane, fell happily and deeply under the sway, at the same time, of Hyde Park bohemian Minna K. Weissenbach, an "opium eater" who hired Young as a secretary and introduced her to such visitors as Thornton Wilder—who taught at the university during the 1930s—and Gertrude Stein. Young would watch "the opium lady" pass into trances and listen to her "speak her dreams aloud." The consequences for Young? "You couldn't live in the opium lady's house and think the rational *was* important."

At Chicago, George Steiner, "having come from a pure French classical lycée tradition," soon "discovered jazz *and* Caesar salad" and learned to play poker—with Hugh Hefner. Steiner's roommate, "an ex-paratrooper and a war veteran who thought I was the funniest, silliest little thing on two legs . . . decided to educate me in fundamental ways. He was streetwise. . . . I owe him a great deal." All this in an atmosphere charged with "an almost physical whiff of supreme quality"—the university's.

If a single influence dominates the talk, it is that of Robert Hutchins, president of the university from 1929 to 1951. At Chicago, as Steiner reflects, "no one had to apologize for intellectual passions," and Hutchins embodied the creed. "His abrasiveness, his arrogance of intellect, his wonderful energy—his 'I-can-do-anything' attitude—that was Hutchins," Steiner says. Directly or indirectly, Hutchins seems to have informed the lives and work of some of our best writers.

One sign of the Hutchins legacy is critical attitude and appetite. Coover took, and takes, pleasure in "disturbing the dogmas," and as a teacher himself feels "the need to reshape the curriculum all the time." Kurt Vonnegut studied anthropology at the university, and, he says, "my ironic distance as a novelist has a lot to do with having been an anthropology student. Anthropology made me a cultural relativist, which is what everybody ought to be."

For Simic, who studied literature, anthropology began close to home: "One of the temptations for an immigrant is to outdo the natives—to immediately get a three-piece suit and read Henry James. It seemed too genteel. I wanted something gutsy, fast, full of anger." He came to reject the "WASPy circles of very informed young men and women who were graduate students. . . . You'd sense that their dream was to be British." So, too, June Jordan, who left the university angry—but full of energy and conviction. The poet Nathaniel Tarn, who studied anthropology at Chicago as a Fulbright fellow, has concluded: "The poet is oppressed by the canon-making academic, who sits in judgment." And Morris Philipson has raised a fundamental question: "I don't think there's any place for a novelist in a university community. . . . At least they don't throw stones."

Writers can make good judges, as a reader or a listener will learn. I wish this book were twice as long, that some who aren't in it were loudly present, and that those who are will be heard. The work of editing someone else's words is always hazardous; both guesswork and the editor's judgment must come into it, and mine have.

Though the preoccupation of this book is writers and Chicago, with the writers responding to details of teachers and ideas and eras, its underlying concern is timeless and general: the making of a writer—or, in this case, twenty-one writers. I hope that the twenty-one self-portraits will be viewed in a generously expansive and dynamic intellectual context, that of twentieth-century American literary vocation, both self-taught and otherwise.

For suggestions and help along the way, in addition to everyone in this book, I must thank Michael Anania, James Atlas, David Brooks, Don Bruckner, Jean Eckenfels, Barbara Epstein, Joseph Epstein, Penelope Kaiserlian, Jonathan Kleinbard, Christine Newman, Edward Rothstein, Brent Staples, and Albert Tannler.

Molly McQuade

Saul Bellow

by Janis Bellow

Saul Bellow was born in 1915 in Lachine, Quebec, Canada, and moved
to Chicago when he was nine. He attended the University of Chicago
from 1933 to 1935, then earned a B.S. with honors in sociology and
anthropology from Northwestern University in 1937. He has taught
at N.Y.U., Princeton University, the University of Minnesota, and
as a member of the Committee on Social Thought at the University
of Chicago.

His many novels include three recipients of the National Book
Award: *The Adventures of Augie March* (Viking, 1953); *Herzog* (Viking, 1964); and *Mr. Sammler's Planet* (Viking, 1970). *Humboldt's Gift*
won both the Pulitzer Prize and the Nobel Prize for Literature in
1976. Bellow received the Gold Medal of the American Academy of
Arts and Letters in 1977.

SAUL BELLOW *Cloudy yearnings*

Q: You came to the University of Chicago when you were how old?

A: I was seventeen, I think.

Q: Tell me your first impressions—of the quadrangles, of teachers, of students, of Hyde Park.

A: I had no idea that Chicago contained anything so grand as the quandrangles. Chicago was different altogether. It was ruder, cruder, noisier, dirtier, grosser, wildly energetic.

Q: And what about your first meetings with teachers?

A: Well, I was terribly puzzled by the arrangements. I didn't understand where to go, what to do. It took me more than a month to find out where the reserve reading room was. For the survey courses, we were handed bundles of books wrapped in twine.

Q: Did you begin to read immediately?

A: I began at once to read them all in the wrong order, seduced by promising titles. Books in social science and biology. We trooped from lecture hall to lecture hall, and were tutored in small groups once a week. I studied poetry with Walter Blair, a stocky, mustached, growling, warm man, and I studied French with Otto F. Bond, from whom I actually learned quickly to read and even to stammer a bit of French. The most memorable survey course lecturers were Professor Carlson, the physiologist, and Louis Wirth, the sociologist.

Q: Why were they memorable?

A: Carlson rolled up the sleeve of his long underwear to drain blood. In Wirth, I encountered my first highly cultivated German Jew, who pronounced each exquisite syllable of every difficult word.

Q: What about student friends? Did you know Isaac then?

A: Of course I did. Isaac Rosenfeld and Oscar Tarcov, Tuley graduates, were my closest friends. Our group was presently joined by Herbert Passin and Irving Janis. Our political friends were Ithiel Pool, George Reedy, and any number of young people from New York's "Ethical Culture School." We Tuley-ites were not dormitory types. We rented gorgeously sleazy rooms for three dollars a week and ate our dinners on 63rd Street where el-trains rattled. The blue plate special of liver and onions with a dessert of Jello or Kosto was served for thirty-five cents. We also haunted the movie houses there and on 55th Street (in the days before it was widened).

Q: What about the bookstores?

A: Well, there were fine secondhand bookstores everywhere. I was especially happy at the Clark and Clark shop, east of the I.C. on 57th Street. The Clark wife was a gangling charmer; the husband was surly but knew his books. There were many old buildings in the neighborhood with sagging corridors and ancient elevators which had to be manned with ropes like three-mast sailing vessels. In Kootich Castle on Harper Avenue there were nonacademic bohemians— artists, photographers, Art Institute pupils, and so on. We undergraduates were shrewdly argumentative, tender with each other. We discussed and wrote poems, stories, plays, and treatises instead of class assignments.

Q: In those days were you aware of the new plan—the Hutchins plan for educational reforms?

A: We seldom bothered our heads about such stuff. Except to laugh about being white mice. We would say, "Vex not thy soul with dry philosophy." Still, we matter-of-factly assumed that the education we were getting was surely the best available. We were not a practical lot. Not even the Depression could make pragmatists or ambitious connivers of us. Of course, Hutchins was our man—we took that for granted. He was fine to look at. He spoke with force and dignity. Just a shade of "put-on" about his incomparable WASP grandeur. We looked upon him with the eyes of Marxists and revolutionists. Hutchins we understood to be an Aristotelian and a Thomist. But it was our conviction that in the four survey courses, we were being taught everything there was to know. We were wildly excited—ecstatic. We had gotten away from home, you see. I realize now that I was grieving for my mother, who had died a year earlier. It's now quite clear to me that I was holding down the pain I felt at her death. I was what people now call a young adult. In those days it never occurred to the young that they were adolescents. "Adolescent" was not one of our words. I took little interest in "developmental psychology." I thought of myself as a writer.

Q: What were you writing? Was there a novel you carried around with you in your head or in a briefcase? Did you manage to steal time from Aristotle or Shakespeare for your own work?

A: No, no. I was only seventeen.

Q: Yes, but you said you considered yourself a writer. There must have been something . . .

A: Little more than a cloudy yearning. What was *there* was a developing perspective, a special view of the surrounding world—seeing people as characters and reading drama into ordinary happenings.

Q: Did you talk to anyone about this? Were you encouraged by any of your profs?

A: I belonged to a group of young men and women who were also developing in this direction.

Q: A kind of cloudy yearnings club.

A: Perhaps the best way to speak of this is to name some of the writers who, as we now say, turned us on when we were young—Theodore Dreiser and Sherwood Anderson on the American side and Arnold Bennett and H. G. Wells in England. This indicates, I believe, that we were strongly stimulated by the figures in their books. These were men and women in very ordinary circumstances. The writers themselves were like that—self-educated people who had seen a way to electrify their nondescript origins and give an artistic character to the humdrum and the drab.

Q: Were you managing to do this at the U of C?

A: The great advantage of the U of C was that it gave us a cover, a color of legitimacy. In the Wieboldt Lounge we gathered to talk about poetry, the novel, the theater. The quadrangles gave a certain cultural weight to our flimsy or sketchy aspirations. They made the impossible look possible. There were also the stacks of Harper Library, where we had access to everything we wished to read. Professors gave courses on the great writers of the West. What had that to do with the kids filling the classrooms? Simply, everything in the world. Professors were there mainly to talk about these things. Our mad intention was to *do* something about them. The students who gathered in the Wieboldt Lounge to listen to discussions about Eliot, Proust, and Kafka were secretly filled with Napoleonic ambitions. They didn't dare to announce publicly what they so passionately and madly aspired to.

Q: So onlookers would have taken you for an ordinary bunch of undergraduates.

A: I think each of us knew the madness was real. But our familes in Duluth or New Orleans or Topeka would have been alarmed.

Q: Had they known . . .

A: Luckily, they had no way of knowing.

Q: I notice you're not singling yourself out.

A: No, because we were a group. There were quite a few of us—not only Isaac Rosenfeld and Oscar Tarcov, but also Paul Goodman, William Barrett, the famous Edouard Roditi, to name only a few.

Q: Before we leave your student days behind, I want to

ask you to unearth one particularly memorable occasion—a stirring class, a late night walk by the lake, a moment of inspiration in the stacks . . .

A: I remember I was living in a tiny bedroom on 57th Street between Woodlawn and Kimbark. I can remember reading Jacob Wasserman's obituary in the *Tribune*. I wrote a long poem about him. He was a novelist we all admired. I forced a friend of mine to listen to this elegy.

Q: Was it an all-night reading?

A: It was a very long poem. He was more polite than moved, but it was a great moment for me. My room had a leaded glass casement window. It made me feel medieval and German.

Q: What happened to the poem?

A: I'm happy to say it was thrown out with other papers.

Q: Now let's talk about your return to Chicago as a young professor. When did you come back?

A: In 1963 I was brought back to Chicago by Edward Shils and John Nef, and for the next thirty years I was a member of the Committee on Social Thought. I was most decently treated by my new colleagues. David Grene was especially welcoming and considerate. I had previously taught at Minnesota, at Princeton, and at N.Y.U. I was by no means a raw recruit.

Q: Did you always have your office in Room 502 in the Social Sciences building?

A: No, no, I was given the office F. von Hayek had just vacated in the middle of the corridor on the fifth floor.

Q: Were you excited, or were you worried that this would take you away from your writing?

A: I had no anxieties about accepting the job. John Nef had explained to me that we were all gentlemen here—at leisure to follow our inclinations and do our own work.

Q: What was Nef like?

A: He was very clearly a gentleman—I was only an apprentice. He was a dark man, quite tall, with a face creased with an habitual smile and large dark eyes that examined you with somber fixity and were half inclined to give up on you —a very European sort of American, entrenched in high culture—and speaking of people I had never heard of. Hyphenated French names like "Bourbon-Busset."

Q: Did you get to know David Grene right away?

A: Yes. I soon came to know David Grene and Marshall Hodgson, the Arabist, who entertained his guests with large bricks of Neapolitan ice cream. Hodgson was a vegetarian, an athlete, and a Quaker. In spite of his marked seriousness, he got into the pen with his two small daughters and played with great earnestness. He never used the elevator but ran up the five flights of stairs. I was saddened by his death. He died running, you know—he was jogging in Stagg Field on a torrid July day.

Q: What did you teach with David Grene in those early years?

A: We did Joseph Conrad, Dickens, Tolstoy, and a great deal of Shakespeare. Our relations were cheerful and affectionate, and I quickly came to respect his critical judgment and his minute knowledge of the texts. Entering the classroom, he often looked as though he had just ridden into town from the Forest Preserves and tethered his horse to the mailbox. Very wisely David taught only half the year. In March he flew back to Ireland in time for the fox hunts.

Q: Were there lunches and after-class gatherings with David Grene at Jimmy's then?

A: Yes. Our local haunt was Jimmy's on 55th Street, a joint I had known in earlier times.

Q: I wonder if I could ask you to give some thumbnail sketches of your other colleagues. What about Hannah Arendt, Victor Turner, Harold Rosenberg?

A: We had any number of stars in the Committee. Let's begin with Hannah Arendt, who for some years came regularly and taught classics with David Grene and lectured on political theory to crowded classrooms. There was a touch of Marlene Dietrich about her. In her manner she was like a Weimar cabaret entertainer. She marched up and down the lecture platform handsomely dressed, often in shortish skirts that showed her legs to advantage. They were youthful and shapely. It was her habit to swing the heavy beads of a long necklace as she terrifically made her points. Fools were not gladly suffered. At times I felt that I was one of them and she was charitably lecturing me about things she didn't believe I knew. She used to tell me how Faulkner should be read. In moments of fatigue she ever so slightly resembled the great George Arliss in the role of Disraeli.

Q: Did you quarrel openly with her?

A: No. I sometimes challenged her, but I was soon aware that there wasn't a single thing that I could possibly tell her.

Q: Shall we move on to Victor Turner?

A: I immensely enjoyed the company and the instructive conversation of the late Victor Turner and his wife Edie. He taught anthropology in the Committee, and other subjects as well. There was a touch of the Music Hall about him, too. He was a pleasant and comfortable round man and a great anecdotalist and drinking companion. He and his wife had lived for years with an African tribe called, if I remember correctly, the Ndembu, who often cropped up in conversation, especially when some very fine point had to be made about liminality—one of his theoretical specialties. I learned a great deal of Midlands slang from him and a vast amount of important gossip.

Q: And Harold Rosenberg. Did you bring him to the Committee?

A: Oh, yes. Harold Rosenberg I had known years earlier in Greenwich Village. He was large-limbed, regal, and handsome, and he walked with a rocking gait. He had been hospitalized with a bone disorder when he was quite young, and was ever so slightly gimpy.

Q: Did you ever teach with him?

A: Yes, I did. I was very fond of him. Let me be downright, I loved him. He was extraordinarily gifted and impressive. In the Village he was known as a distinguished "idea" man—chief theoretician of the Tenth Street school of painters (de Kooning, Saul Steinberg, Baziotes), a contributor to the *Partisan Review* in its best days. He was also a secret power in some strange way in the advertising world—a one-man think tank, subsidized by the Advertising Council. He went there to read the papers, study politics and history, and write memoranda. Of course he was a Marxist, and a subtle one. The Advertising Council got good value out of him.

Q: So what did he do in Chicago?

A: In the Committee he taught beautiful courses on literature, painting, politics. He was a high-minded man who was also deeply shrewd. Nothing petty about Harold. His conspicuous mustache was matched by a bar of expressive eyebrows. He was on principle totally unsentimental, and if you were going to get into a conversation with him, you had better not try to fake anything. He would flatten you scornfully if he spotted you as a phony. A great Francophile, he particularly admired Paul Valéry. When I first knew him on Second Avenue and in Washington Square Park, it soon became obvious that in his early days he had been a Leninist and that he would have been capable of having people eliminated. Since he couldn't *really* have anybody shot, he substituted humor for firepower! See his essay, "A Herd of Independent Minds." He was a fine man whom I valued greatly and still argue with in secret.

Q: Were there others?

A: Oh yes, there were many distinguished figures in the Committee—Frank Knight, Hans Jonas, Dolf Sternberger. If I were writing a book, I would devote a chapter to each of them—several chapters to Edward Shils alone. But I shall never have the time for it, what with my days flying faster than the weaver's shuttle.

Q: The university neighborhood has changed greatly, I understand.

A: I find it still gives me pleasure to recall the look of Hyde Park in the old days: the 55th streetcar turning into Lake Park and swinging into Harper Avenue, where the conductor got out in front of Kootich Castle to pull down one trolley and raise the other. I had friends and even a cousin or two in the seedy castle. I have never lost my feeling for those odd corners of the neighborhood. Rosenberg often accused me of sentimentality. He would say, "Watch it! Watch it!" I do have much too clear a recollection of the many shabby tenements where we lived, my friends and I. The friends are gone, and so are the slums that housed them.

Q: In closing, let's turn to your last decade on the Committee and in particular your friends from that time.

A: David Grene and Allan Bloom, my dearest friends in the Committee, enjoyed (if that is the word) a reputation for oddity. In neither case could I see this as anything but normalcy in a higher form—beyond the reach of casual observers. Yes, David Grene unfailingly returned to his crops and his cattle and his buddies in Derrycark [Ireland], while Bloom flew to Paris as often as possible. Bloom was not only a rigorous and systematic thinker, he was also a comic genius. It's impossible to do justice to the man in a brief interview. To do justice to him, moreover, I would need to know what he knew, and I would never satisfactorily reproduce his learning. At least not without divine intervention—a supernatural crash course, or revelation. Here I have only intuition to rely on.

Q: And a superb memory. I'm sure that your readers would like to hear about the classes that the two of you taught together.

A: Well, Allan had developed an interest in the famous novels of the eighteenth and nineteenth century. Even the twentieth. We taught Proust and Céline's *Journey to the End of Night*. We devoted a term also to Joyce's *Ulysses*.

Q: You did Gide too, and also read T. S. Eliot and Svevo's *Confessions of Zeno* and Dickens and Shakespeare and Nietzsche. You taught together for nearly a dozen years.

A: Yes, we did all that. Allan had not read many novels previously. I converted him. He began to say that novelists were, after all, the best phenomenologists.

Q: We students saw in all this a living demonstration of the lines drawn between literature and philosophy. A fair exchange—your Dostoyevsky and Flaubert for his Plato and Machiavelli.

A: It sounds like National League trading! One shortstop for two outfielders.

Q: We laughed a lot in those classes, too. The seminars never felt heavy or academic.

A: We continued in the classroom the conversations we began at lunch.

Q: There always seemed to be a large emotional charge in those exchanges. Many of us sat on the edge of our seats when the big guns began to go off.

A: Allan was never hard on me. He put up with my ignorance and obstinacy. I felt that he was gently educating me.

Q: He also had a way of drawing you out by asking simple questions.

A: You will remember with what elegance he entered the classroom, dressed by Armani, Hermès, and Lanvin, and put his beloved toys on the table: his gold Mont Blanc pen, his gold Dunhill lighter, his state-of-the-art wristwatch.

Q: With a cup of espresso before him, he might have been at the Café Flor in Paris.

A: Yeah! But there was nothing conspicuous or showy about him. Through an open shirt-button you saw the old Adam. He adored spending money on trifles. His bearing and the assumptions he made about himself, his unrestrained frankness set him apart from everybody else in the university community. He despised the Woolworth variety of chicken-feed opinion and the stratagems of academic departmental meetings. He took a lot of heat from his colleagues because his students, seeing that he could put some real order into their confused lives, were extraordinarily loyal to him. Many professors—a mite rivalrous perhaps—found this hard to forgive.

Q: I remember the crowds that turned up to hear him lecture on *The Republic* or *Emile*. Standing room only.

A: Yes, while he lighted cigarettes with a shaking hand and burnt holes in his Ultimo neckties. You always felt you were in the presence of the real Bloom. There was no supporting cast or auxiliary personnel. The kids would say: "He's for real." They were absolutely right.

Paul Carroll

The poet Paul Carroll, Chicago-born, received an M.A. from the University of Chicago in 1952. He was poetry editor of the *Chicago Review* and editor of *Big Table* magazine. Until 1993 he taught at the University of Illinois at Chicago. He then resigned from Illinois with the rank of professor emeritus of English and moved with his wife to a farm in North Carolina. His collections of poetry include *New and Selected Poems* (Yellow Press, 1978), *The Garden of Earthly Delights* (Chicago Office of Fine Arts, 1987), *Poems & Psalms* (Big Table Books, 1991), and *The Beaver Dam Road Poems* (Big Table Books, 1994). He has finished a collection of literary anecdotes called "Straight Poets I Have Known and Loved."

Carroll formerly lived in a loft on Chicago's West Side. As the interview proceeded, we sat smeared with sunlight, startling and urban. Sculpture and sculptural equipment—his wife's—occupied parts of the loft, casually monumental, and there was a lot of wine.

Carroll talks with bravado and broad charm. This was not a chore but a sincere performance, theatrically effusive. And generous. The talk continued, and it continued.

PAUL CARROLL *A student*
in Plato's academy

In the Catholic faith there is a tradition of seven heavens. St. Paul, for example, in one of his epistles, speaks of himself as having been taken up into the third heaven, where apparently he had extraordinary experiences. Three of the heavens I have known in my own life are the Catholic Church, the University of Chicago, and the most glorious heaven of all: good poetry.

Both the Church and the university, certainly, have contributed to whatever poetry I have been able to write, for each in its own way held up as an example the dignity and the mystery of human nature and thought. Each also encouraged a sense of human freedom.

But this doesn't ask the poet to propagandize for a humanistic ideal of any kind; it encourages the poet to believe in the reality of his own experience and feelings when he is given a poem to write. The heaven of the Church and the University of Chicago helped me to realize the heaven of poetry, to explore it, and not to kowtow or conform. The atmosphere at the university was of an intense and very happy intellectual adventure. The premium was on independent thought.

For a poet, every day is the beginning of the world. You're in the Garden of Eden every morning—it's as simple as that—and the animals have not been named. All we know is, there's a strange voice out there; sometimes it yells at us, but mostly it's friendly. That same sense of freedom and wonder we know of from the myths of the Garden of Eden, a poet knows every day. The U of C and the Church helped me to realize that this could be true in poetry.

My Chicago experience began with Robert Maynard Hutchins, who was very kind to me.

I came from Hyde Park and Flossmoor; I'd lived in both places and gone to grammar school at St. Thomas Apostle. At St. Thomas, the U of C was sort of a joke, because their football teams were so awful. I loved athletics, basketball particularly, and I used to go to Stagg Field on Saturdays to see how badly they'd be beaten.

After St. Thomas, I went to a South-Side Catholic high school, Mount Carmel—a big jock school, a prep school for future Notre Dame athletes. The Mount Carmel priests and nuns used to tell us that the U of C was an atheistic, Communistic place. (Which, of course, wasn't true at all! The great Thomist revival had begun at the University in the late 1930s.)

When I got through with the navy in 1946, the competition to get into college was fierce; many more guys than usual were able to go because of the GI Bill. So I couldn't get into Notre Dame, and I went to Illinois Wesleyan instead.

The only thing I liked about Wesleyan was that it was near the country; I could take walks. I didn't give a fuck about classes until, for reasons I still can't quite understand, in the spring of my freshman year I began to read books. Suddenly I couldn't get enough of them.

Nothing in my background had prepared me for this, although my father loved to read Burns and Shakespeare. There wasn't much stimulation in my background as far as art went, and Illinois Wesleyan certainly didn't stimulate me. It was a small Methodist school; we had to go to chapel every day. I came from a Catholic world, and I thought, "What *is* this?" They thought God was a life insurance salesman.

I knew that this school wasn't for me, but I didn't know what to do. There was no one I could talk to. And so my father, who knew and supported Hutchins, wrote him, asking if I could go to see him.

It was the spring of 1947 when I went. At the time, Hutchins had one office at the university, where he was chancellor, and another at the *Encyclopaedia Britannica* headquarters, where he was editor in chief. That's where I went, down in the old *Daily News* building near the Northwestern Station in the Loop.

I'll never forget his office, spacious and quite elegant. Hutchins came from around the desk, almost knocking me over. He was very tall, very handsome, and very dapper. Total charm. Jesus.

He said to me, "What can I do to make you happy?"

I almost fainted. I was nineteen. No one had ever asked me that before.

I told him I'd begun to read books, loved them, and didn't know what to do.

He said, "Where do you go to school?"

"Illinois Wesleyan."

"Get out of there *immediately*. Go somewhere where you will learn something and meet other students who love books, too. Go to Harvard or Princeton, or go to my old school, Yale, or to Columbia. Or of course, come here—come to the U of C. You're from Hyde Park. Come home."

What I liked about him was not so much his graciousness as that there was no bullshit. He didn't give a speech about how small schools have their place, that kind of nonsense. And he said, "Please let me know what you decide."

So of course I went to the U of C.

My first year there was disastrous. I had to take courses I hated, like natural sciences and German and mathematics—which I flunked.

The university was going to throw me out. They said,

"You must take this math course a second time and pass it. Otherwise, you *will* be expelled."

So I went back to Cobb Hall in the winter of 1949 to take the class again, and guess who's there? The same teacher. A young, passionate mathematician. It was a small class, eight or ten students. And the teacher said to me—I always sat in the back—"Are *you* here again?"

I told him yes. He had given me an F because I was so dumb. I still couldn't understand much. I tried hard.

And on a day I will never forget I became a U of C student.

The teacher was talking about some theorems of Pascal. I raised my hand, and he said, "*You* have a question?" It was the first question I'd ever asked.

I said, "Yes. Is that the same Pascal who wrote the great book about his thoughts, the *Pensées?*" The Pascal I loved was the mystic.

The teacher threw a fit. "Yes," he said, "Pascal was a great mathematician; some of his theorems are still in use. He was a genius in science. He was also an inventor. Then he gave it up for that crazy mysticism."

I said, "Pascal wrote, 'The heart has reasons of its own that reason has no knowledge of.'"

By now he was in a rage.

I said, "Pascal wrote, 'The silence of these infinite spaces terrifies me.'"

He said, "That has nothing to do with mathematics!"

I passed the class, just squeaked through with a C minus, but I passed. Then, after that year was over, I had a great time at Chicago.

Several wonderful teachers in the English department taught me. My favorites were Norman Maclean, Napier Wilt, and J. V. Cunningham.

Some of the other teachers at the U of C were boring, boring, boring. They were so *pompous*. Smart men, but teaching was all a big thing about themselves and how much they knew. They didn't talk about the books as Wilt or Maclean did. Wilt and Maclean and Cunningham had passion. I'll always remember them.

Maclean flunked me. He was one of the best things that ever happened to me.

I loved him because he would read a passage from Shakespeare, give a wolf whistle, and say, "That's writing, pal." And you would sit there terrified. Or he would read Hopkins, and get up and go look out the window, and he wouldn't say anything.

I had him my first year in graduate school in English in an introduction to Shakespeare course. His final exam was an essay. I admired Maclean and wanted to impress him. His test questions were basic: "Describe the plot of *Hamlet*" and that sort of thing. So I decided to show off. I thought, "I'll write a prose poem." Free association, like Joyce.

It was Maclean's tradition to go over the exams with us in class and explain his grading system. I turned up convinced that I was going to get a gold star. He said, "This was one of the most unusual sets of exams I've had in many years of teaching—it included the best paper I've ever received and the worst."

Without giving names, he read the best paper—and it wasn't mine. I was stunned. Then he read the worst. It was mine. He flunked me. I hated him for a whole year.

I took the class again the next fall quarter, and got an A, because I answered the questions the way you are supposed to.

That was a lesson. I teach my students the lesson today: just do the best you can and don't show off, no matter what.

J. V. Cunningham was also a good teacher, and he wrote some fine epigrams. He was the great iconoclast of the department.

He wasn't a neo-Aristotelian, you see. That was the rage then. I could never quite understand what the neo-Aristotelians were talking about. Truly. I didn't care about literary theory.

Cunningham used to lie in wait for students in his class on Shakespeare and Ben Jonson. All the students in those years—everyone, even the nursing students—began the fall quarter by reading Aristotle's *Poetics*. So Cunningham would wait for the students to come in, and he'd read a passage from Shakespeare, and say, "Smith . . . What did you feel about this thing? Smith?" And Smith would say, "Pity and fear."

Cunningham, very tall, would come around from behind his desk—it was really rather cruel—and stand over Smith and say, "Did you really feel pity? And what did you say? *Fear?*" The young neo-Aristotelian had never been challenged before.

Cunningham was like a good broom: he loved literature, and he swept it clean. He was more cynical than Maclean, like a spoiled Jesuit or a disillusioned lover, disappointed by the world. But he taught me a lot.

Another great teacher was Napier Wilt, who became dean of humanities. Maclean was very short, stocky, a jock type—he could have been a lightweight boxer. He loved to play pool and drink. He was very Scottish. But Wilt was an enormous whale of a creature, huge! He liked to wear a belt *and* suspenders, in the old style. He was completely bald; he looked like an egg. He was a famous gourmet and a distinguished homosexual. And he had a secondhand Rolls-Royce that he used to drive around in.

The reason I loved him was that he was a terrific teacher of Henry James and Walt Whitman. I would go to visit him in his office. Since my own adviser could never remember my name, I got Napier to be a kind of surrogate adviser.

We got on well because we liked the same things in

literature. I'd go up to see him on some summer day, and he'd be stretched out in his office, with his *huge* stomach, and he'd have this little Modern Library book on the stomach. It was like a small bird on a whale. And he'd say, "Carroll, I've just been rereading *Wuthering Heights*." Then he would talk about the characters as if they were real people. He made them live for you.

Sadness later entered my relations with Wilt. While he was dean and I was an editor of the *Chicago Review*, a scandal erupted about an issue of the magazine, and my friend Irving Rosenthal, editor of the *Review*, had to consult with Wilt about it in his capacity as dean. Wilt was embarrassed about the whole thing; though he was a spokesman for the university, which considered us troublemakers, he believed we had done no wrong.

I've been in disgrace at the university for many years because of my part in the scandal and because of establishing *Big Table* magazine. But we didn't start *Big Table* to embarrass the university. That wasn't the idea. We began *Big Table* after the university suppressed publication of an issue of the *Chicago Review* while I was an editor there. The issue included a good many Beat writers, which was one reason the university objected to it.

Actually, I was twice on the staff of *CR*. First it was as a student in 1951 or 1952. Then, after I had left the university and was teaching at Notre Dame and the downtown College in 1957, Irving Rosenthal got in touch with me. "How would you like to be poetry editor of the *Review?*" he asked.

I said, "I can't be, because I'm not a student."

He said, "Then I appoint you *guest* poetry editor." So I joined the *Review* again in 1957, and was on the staff until 1959, when we all quit. I started *Big Table* in 1959.

What were our intentions as editors? Just to publish good literature, like any little magazine: publish what is new, as well as what is old. We had no intention of being a Beat magazine. I published some of the Beat writers, but I published many other writers, too, like Updike and Mailer. The idea was to publish only what seemed genuine and real, and stick to our guns.

I learned from Maclean, from Cunningham, and from Napier Wilt; I also learned from McKeon.

Oh, he was a passionate, humorous, dedicated man who loved his subject. I took a class with him, and got an A, in Aristotle!

McKeon had an interesting background. The name is Irish, and his mother was Jewish, so he looked like Karl Shapiro, both Jewish and Irish. And he wasn't a Catholic, but he had an enormous enthusiasm and respect for Catholic thinking. His real hero was Aristotle, and he also taught Plato well. The only drawback was, he wrote poorly.

By the time I went to study with McKeon, I knew a little bit about St. Thomas and the others. One reason I did was that a friend of my mother's, a convert to Catholicism, had gotten after me about the Church. I never liked her. There's nothing worse than a convert, nothing.

I had left the Church, you see, in 1950 or so, but my mother's friend got to my intellectual vanity. She said, "I think you should have the dignity to find out what you've left." And of course I said, "Okay." She persuaded me to take a weekly study session at the Albertus Magnus House of Studies in River Forest. Dominican monks lived there (Aquinas had been a Dominican). Said this lady, friend of my mother, "There are many converts among the monks who were once University of Chicago students."

So for two or three years I went to River Forest every week. Took a long train ride from the U of C to the end of the Oak Park line and then walked a mile to this big monastery. I did indeed meet a famous former U of C student who had become a monk; his name was Benedict Ashley. He was nice enough to spend time with me. Together we read a lot of St. Thomas and Aristotle.

The Dominicans wanted me to try for at least a year to become a monk. I considered it seriously. For if you're Catholic, you may, as they say, have a vocation. It's a little hard to say, as Joyce did, "*Non serviam.* I refute it all." Who are *you,* you arrogant little soul?

I never felt that kind of arrogance, but I thought to myself, "I don't want to be a monk." And I finally told them, "I'm a poet, and I must keep myself open. I cannot be a Catholic poet. I can't have preconceived ideas. They're a stranglehold."

When I went to study with McKeon, he liked the fact that I knew a bit about St. Thomas and Aristotle. I was still having troubles then with Catholicism, and I used to talk them over with him. He encouraged me to give the Church a chance, but to be very careful not to be taken in by rhetoric or emotion. What he encouraged me to do was to think with my own head. He wasn't against the Church, necessarily; he just wasn't a Catholic.

I liked what I learned from him. He taught me to make up my own mind and think things through as best I could, and not look for an easy, sloganistic answer.

My teachers, though, were not my mentors. They didn't teach me much about poetry. Most of that I learned by myself. My mentors were the poets I was reading: Yeats, Eliot, Hopkins, Rimbaud, Donne, Keats, Neruda, Rilke, St. John Perse. These poets were my uncles, or my brothers. *They* were the family; they were the legacy.

At Chicago I first started to write poetry. I loved poetry but had never considered writing it.

One evening, a fellow student of mine told me that she had fallen in love. Her face glowed. I was stunned. And so I went home and wrote a sonnet, which I laid on her the next day.

She said, "It's bad Hopkins," which it was, "but I'm touched."

I began writing poetry then. Once I'd started, I couldn't stop. My grades began to fall. I became bored with school. All I wanted to do was write poems. This was in 1952. I was twenty-one or twenty-two.

At Chicago I also met some other young poets who were trying their hands at writing. One was Stanley Rosen, a very bright kid from Cleveland. He had published a book called *Death in Egypt* while he was just a student, and I was totally jealous. *Death in Egypt!* How, I wondered, could he have gotten such a concept? Stanley later became a philosopher; he was one of those classic U of C types. He would argue with me over cheesecake, which he ate enormous amounts of—he got very fat—and his girlfriend would be yelling at him, knocking on the window of the restaurant.

All these women knocking on windows and dragging their men away from *me!*

Arthur Heiserman was another student friend of mine. He was a medievalist who eventually became a U of C professor; he died young. Art and I became friends when we were grad students in English. We used to go up to talk in the only quiet place at the university, which was the men's john on the fourth floor of Wieboldt Hall.

There was an anteroom before the door leading to the toilets, and in the anteroom was a hard wooden couch and a filthy Gothic window with the graffiti of ten generations of students on it. We'd sit and talk and pace and smoke, and there was always a faintly urinous smell. We'd talk about the glorious vices of the Roman Catholic Church, and I felt like a medieval student at the University of Paris, or a student in Plato's academy. At that point, Arthur was a good German Lutheran kid from Evansville, Indiana; he was bitterly opposed to the Catholic Church. So we had endless arguments. Neither of us ever won.

The irony is that Arthur later became a convert to the Roman Catholic faith, as did his wife. I left the Church—again. Yet I continued to love one aspect of it: the absolute insistence on an eternal reality, and the idea that we are all immortal beings. That Jesus Christ was born of a virgin is incredible; that's why I believe it. That we are immortal creatures is *inconceivable;* that's why I believe it.

You follow your instincts as best you can, both in writing poetry and in making up your mind about the Catholic Church.

Poetry is a way of knowing; it's one of the great ways of knowing. But the knowledge earned from poetry, and understood partially, is not a kind that can be known beforehand. That's the point. Poetry belongs to that inner world about which we know a lot and we know nothing.

Poets can be quite ignorant. Some are poorly educated, like Dylan Thomas, and others are highly educated, like T. S. Eliot. Thomas was a far better lyric poet than Eliot, so what difference did education make? Eliot was a great poet, in his own way. So what's the difference?

Yet poets all know one thing: that poetry will teach them if they can keep writing it.

From poetry you learn joy and work. One joy is the complete joy of creativity. It *is* complete, though poetry can be hard work as well as great joy. And you learn a sense of awe, since what you write cannot help but be, to use Plato's terms, part of the good, the true, and the beautiful. Poetry also teaches you a profound humility, as though you were a scribe to whom poems were given.

You do not choose poetry. You don't earn it. You don't learn it at any university, including the University of Chicago. It is given to you, and you don't know why.

Hayden Carruth

Hayden Carruth earned an M.A. from the University of Chicago in 1948 and then worked in Chicago as editor-in-chief of *Poetry* magazine (1949–50) and as an associate editor at the University of Chicago Press (1951–52). Until his retirement, he taught at Syracuse University.

Recently the author of *Collected Shorter Poems, 1946–1991* (Copper Canyon Press, 1992), which won a National Book Critics Circle award, Carruth has published many other volumes of poetry and a novel, *Appendix A* (Macmillan, 1963). He is well known as the editor of *The Voice That Is Great within Us: American Poetry of the Twentieth Century* (Bantam, 1970).

A man with an owlish look and an austere bearing, Carruth answers questions with a blunt, thoughtful swing. He seems unhesitating in his willingness to consider ideas. Carruth is firm, insightful, and can be gruff. More than anything else, though, he seems humble about himself, his past, and his prospects.

HAYDEN CARRUTH *Beautiful language*

Suffering is essential to sympathy, and sympathy is essential to poetry. People who haven't suffered are unable to get inside the consciousness of other people. It's not only the consciousness of other people; it's the consciousness of animals and of nature generally. One has to have a kind of fellow feeling. Pain, and the knowledge of pain, not only physical but spiritual pain, is important to any artist. An artist who cannot speak for the pain and suffering of the world is very limited, is not going to do very much.

When I was a student at the University of Chicago, I wished I were somebody else. Oh, almost anybody. I was very ill; I was very unhappy. I felt terribly isolated and cut off, even though I had friends and a wife. I thought that I was nobody, not made for this world. And it was true, in a way. It took me a long, long time to be able to live anything like a normal life.

I became acutely ill while I was still a graduate student at Chicago. One of the things that happened to me was a certain kind of auditory hallucination. It didn't last for very long, but I used to hear soprano voices singing in the trees on campus.

I have never been able to explain this to myself. I'm not a delusionary person. My illness was not of that kind. But it was a matter of tension, I suppose, of anxiety. Sitting in a classroom was often very difficult for me. I would have to sit right next to the door, so I could escape. It was in some of my classes that I heard those voices. I wrote a poem called "I Tell You for Several Years of My Insanity I Heard the Voice of Lilith Singing in the Treetops of Chicago." The poem comes out of that experience.

The quality I remember of the voices in the treetops was unspecific. The voices did not have any musical qualities. It was like the sound of the universe. There were no words. No meaning was attached. I heard just the sound. I didn't hear any specific angels, really.

I was already headed in the direction of poetry before this happened.

I had gone to undergraduate school at the University of North Carolina before the war. In some respects, I received a good education there, and in other respects it was very isolating. Although I was interested in writing, I knew very little about twentieth-century literature—a few of the novelists, perhaps, but hardly any of the poets, although I had been writing poetry for a long time, probably since I was in grammar school.

When I went to Chicago as a veteran in 1946, everything changed. I became almost immediately aware of the artistic, literary, and intellectual life of the mid-twentieth-century period, partly through the university, partly through friends I met, and partly through the bookshops on 57th Street. The whole atmosphere was totally new to me, very lively, very acute. A lot of people were a lot better educated than I was. In a couple of years, I became much more knowledgeable. I became serious about my own work. I began writing a lot.

My family had been writers for two generations before me, though not in the sense that I was a writer or in the sense that any avant-garde, twentieth-century person is a writer. They were mainstream writers making a living at it, as one could in the early days. I was always told that my birth was paid for by a check from the *Saturday Evening Post* for a poem—a piece of light verse.

My grandfather was a humorist in the tradition of Mark Twain; he knew Twain. He wrote comic stories about the American frontier. And he wrote some poetry. (So did my father.) He became an editor and a relatively important literary personage in his time. His name, Hayden Carruth, was the same as mine. Actually, his first name was Fred, but for literary purposes he used Hayden, his middle name. And when I was born, my father wanted to name me after my grandfather, but my mother refused to have a son named Fred. So they called me Hayden.

My father was a newspaper editor. He was self-educated. His taste was very Edwardian, and when he tried to read most contemporary poetry, he disliked it intensely. He was unable to read it, in effect. So we had a considerable division of sensibility. But at the same time, I should say that his interest in poetry, and his interest in me as a neophyte writer, was always important to me. My grandfather's was, too.

I was raised in a radical family. My father was a socialist, my grandfather had been a socialist, and I had studied the history of American and European radicalism when I was quite young. I supported third parties, and that sort of thing, but was never a party member or an actively political person. I just did my writing. I feel that my politics gets into my writing.

My father was very much interested in the pre-Raphaelite poets and the late nineteenth-century poets. He had a pretty good library of that stuff, and when I went to Chicago, those were the poets I knew—Shelley and Keats, Swinburne and Tennyson, and so on. In public school I had been subjected to Longfellow and Bryant and Whittier, but had never read Whitman or Emily Dickinson—they were not taught then. I read poets you've never heard of—Thomas L. Thomas, for instance. But when I was at Chicago and became aware of what was going on in the real world, I lost my interest in most of that. In fact, I can remember my friend Allen Tate, who was older than I, and whom I first met at Chicago—he taught there for a semester, I think—saying that the whole purpose of his generation of poets was to displace the sensibility of Cambridge in 1870 and replace it with something more up-to-date. When I went to the University of Chicago, what I had was the sensibility of Cambridge in 1870.

While I was a student, I thought of myself as a writer. Before I went to Chicago, I thought of myself as a prose writer, primarily. I thought I would be a journalist or a novelist. I took my degree at North Carolina in journalism, and my father and grandfather had basically been in journalism of one kind or another. At Chicago, I decided I was going to be a poet, but I didn't jettison the idea that I would do other kinds of writing. I expected that I would. And in fact, over the course of my life, I have done a little bit of every kind of writing there is. And I've benefited from that. When my students tell me now that they're poets, and they're not going to write anything but poetry, I tell them that's foolish, elitist. You can learn a good deal from writing advertising copy, or jacket copy for books, or speeches. I've done a lot of ghostwriting. It all goes together; it *all* helps.

At first, I didn't know that I was a poet, but I knew that I *wanted* to be a poet, and that became a conscious aim while I was a student at Chicago. About six months after I got there, I decided that's what I wanted to do, that's what I would give my attention to—and I did.

I was writing; I was trying to write. I was working at it, I was not being very successful in my own mind, but nevertheless I *was* producing some poems that seemed to me to have possibilities. I enjoyed it. I felt it was important—much more so then than now, in a way. People like Eliot and Pound and Williams seemed to have had a really big influence on American culture. They were important people. And what they did was what I wanted to do. I gave up any idea of being a journalist, although I did a lot of book reviews, and that kind of thing, for newspapers. But I didn't do anything else. And that was a conscious decision.

I can't remember the instant when I made it, but I can remember the period when I was making it.

I'd given up ambitions to do anything else. It was a joyous decision, but also fearful, because I was afraid of asserting myself, and writing poetry is a kind of self-assertion. But I did it anyway.

At that time, Chicago was a wonderful place for European scholars and writers and artists—refugees, mostly—who had been invited to come to the University by Bob Hutchins. They brought to Chicago a kind of European pitch, I would say, a pitch of intellectual endeavor, that hasn't always been associated with American intellectual life. They influenced a lot of people—people like Paul Goodman, and Saul Bellow, and so on—who were a little older than I, but whom I knew at least slightly. They set the tone for the whole campus, I think.

Hutchins was a mythological kind of guy. I think he cultivated the myth himself. He was very smart, and he had a *practical* vision. He was not an idealist, but he had a vision of what the university could do for the rest of the community, for the rest of the nation, that I don't find today in the academy. I don't find it. Instead, I find a lot of administrators who are worried sick about money and who are spending all their time fooling around with budgets, and that's it. There *aren't* any great university presidents anymore.

Hutchins was one, and he produced a remarkable university. It didn't last, but his idea that one could create an educational institution that would carry people through from kindergarten to the Ph.D. and give them a truly integrated education was important.

I met Paul Goodman when he was visiting Chicago, and we became friends—not close friends, but pretty good friends. He was a voracious intellect, interested in everything. He was a monomaniacal kind of guy; he talked all the time, wouldn't let anybody else say anything. He was opinionated, and so dogmatic and so rude sometimes that he could enrage you quite easily. But I always got along all right with him. I didn't have any big arguments with him. I was willing to listen to him. I always admired him greatly. I admire his poetry *a lot*. He was a fascinating talker, another of those people who seemed to me brilliant and knowledgeable. And I think he was a pretty good product of the University of Chicago of the 1940s. He learned a lot from people like Richard McKeon, and others there, and carried on that tradition. Goodman was the kind who always reacted *against* whatever was presented to him. He was very tough and independent.

I knew Bellow at Chicago. I knew him better later on, in New York, but I met him first in Chicago. He was another one of these guys like Goodman—he was an intellect, not simply a writer. He was interested in ideas. He worked very hard. He lived hard. In his younger days, in his books up to and including *Henderson the Rain King*, he was really productive, doing a lot of good work. I don't think people nowadays appreciate him the way he ought to be appreciated.

People like McKeon, in the philosophy department, were first-rate. Rudolf Carnap was also in the philosophy department; I remember working with him. Jacques Maritain was around, though I don't know if he ever actually taught there. And there was a fellow named Rexford Tugwell, who had been a member of Roosevelt's administration in Washington. He was an early city planner who was associated with Lewis Mumford. When I first went to Chicago, I thought I was going to be a social scientist, and so I took a course from Tugwell. He was a wonderful person. He was full of ideas, full of *new* ideas—the kind of person who, when you talked with him, was a stimulation and an inspiration.

In the English department, I was particularly influenced by Norman Maclean, although I didn't know it at the time. The courses I took from him were very enlightening. The most important was a course in literary theory, starting with Bergson and Croce and going on down to Eliot and John Crowe Ransom and the New Critics. I read a lot of stuff in that course that was important to me, even though it was all theory. It wasn't poetry, but it opened up my mind to all kinds of speculation about literature and art and life and experience.

As a graduate student, I was very much influenced by the New Critics. But after I left Chicago, I began to think that the New Criticism was limited and somewhat dangerous. By concentrating all their attention on the explication of the text, the New Critics eliminated—not *always,* but in extreme cases—any connection between the text and the rest of experience, which seemed to me to lead to the position that there is no way to judge a poem in moral terms, only in aesthetic terms. And I felt that was wrong. After I left Chicago, I was very much influenced by the European existentialist writers of the mid-century period; I was very much influenced by Camus and Sartre, and by their feeling that a writer had to be engaged and responsible, and that the relationship between literature and experience was close and functional, went both ways. So I began, in my own work, to write in that way—less aimed toward the creation of a perfect work of art and more aimed toward a document or an expression that would be socially useful.

Napier Wilt was a teacher who helped me a good deal. And I took a course on Eliot from Williamson—a very thorough exploration not only of Eliot but of his ideas and methods and how he related to other people of his time, like Pound. I learned a lot from that class. The poet Jim Cunningham—J. V. Cunningham—taught it, and he and I were close friends. And the chairman of the English department, a neo-Aristotelian who had quite a reputation, was Ronald Crane—he was a member of Richard McKeon's group, as was Elder Olson, also of the English department. I liked Crane and his wife; I spent a lot of time talking to them. I can't remember who all the other people were. There was a wonderful medievalist named Hulbert who taught me Chaucer and Middle English and philology—the kinds of courses we all had to take in those days. I found them fascinating. From childhood, I had always been fascinated by language. The more I learned about it, the better I liked it.

The first modern poet I read was William Carlos Williams. *The Collected Poems of William Carlos Williams* was one of the first books I bought, with my small GI allowance, after I got to Chicago. It had been published in 1939, so of course it didn't contain the poems Williams wrote after 1939 that were so important. But still, it was a big event in my life to read that book.

I don't know if the book changed my life, but it changed my writing enormously. I studied Williams's language, his metric, and tried to figure out what he was doing. I never really did. But at least I became acquainted with possibilities that had been closed to me before. And from there I went on and read Stevens and Pound and Eliot and e. e. cummings and a whole bunch of others, many of them now mostly forgotten.

Pound was very important to me. He was a problem to me, as he is to almost everybody, because I couldn't agree with many of his ideas. Nevertheless, I found his talents, his skill, his lyrical ability, and his whole manner of writing very attractive. And of course, he was terribly important in the evolution of twentieth-century literature. He was a forerunner of and a big influence on almost everybody. Years later, when I edited an anthology called *The Voice That Is Great within Us,* I dedicated it to Pound—not so much for myself as for all of us. It was a gesture by the whole community toward him.

One could, however, become oppressed by the example of Pound, who did so much, wrote so much, was such an influence, was so widely read, knew so many languages. If I had let myself be too influenced, I would have simply been intimidated, and I wouldn't have made any progress at all. In order to make progress, I had to reject him, or at least I had to stand up and say, "I can do what *I* do just as well as you did what you did." That's a daring and reckless thing to do, for many people, anyway; it certainly was for me. But it had to be done, and I suppose it involved a kind of hatred, a kind of rebellion, certainly.

I felt—and, in a way, I still feel—that the great poets of the first half of the century were towering figures that we could never equal. Other people felt that way, too. It was quite a common feeling. I think every poet has to over-come the work of the people preceding him, has to come to terms with it. (When I went to live in New England years later, I had the same problem with Robert Frost, as every New England poet does.) You have to bury the old guys somehow, and still go on and do your own thing despite the fact that they put their imprint so powerfully on litera-ture. The poets who came along just before me also had a big influence on me—Karl Shapiro, Randall Jarrell, Robert Lowell, Delmore Schwartz. They were not much older than I, but they had already established themselves by the time I came to Chicago, and their opinions and their ways of writing were something that I had to overcome. That's part of the process of becoming a writer.

Winfield Townley Scott was a poet whose work I liked quite a lot at Chicago and whom nobody reads at all any-more, as far as I know. Scott had a way of using tradition in contemporary language, and he had a sense of beauty. Most of these poets had a sense of beauty. You don't see it very much anymore; I don't find it in my students at all. But it was always important to me. I was very much influ-enced by Yeats, as well as by Pound, and the thing that attracted me was simply that they wrote beautiful language.

By beautiful language I mean expressive language. (It's

a term I use in my teaching.) It certainly does not have anything to do with prettiness or necessarily with musicality in language, or anything like that. It's language that is heightened and truly expressive of emotion. That's what I call the beautiful. I always—or much of the time—try to write that way myself.

Beauty can be a very subtle thing. It can be something that other people don't even recognize. But I've always had it in my mind.

Beauty also always has an element of communal feeling in it. The addresses of Martin Luther King, for instance, strike me as beautiful, even though they serve a very immediate political and social purpose. Some poetry has also done that. Everyone acknowledges that one of Pound's most beautiful works is the 45th canto, about usury. The poem is generated by political and social feeling, and at the same time it is eloquent. The language is certainly beautiful.

At Chicago, I was required to think all the time—that was the whole point of the university, especially in that period. So I did a lot of that. And I do believe that analysis and thought can enhance one's reading of a poem, although I suspect that people who can respond intuitively, without any need to intellectualize, probably enjoy it more. When I was a student in graduate school, however, I would say that I was doing both things equally—thinking and understanding. They were interconnected, not divorced.

We did have theorists in the English department—the neo-Aristotelians—who were serious about their theoretical conjectures, but we did not have people who were the kind of theorists with a capital "t" who inhabit the English departments today; they didn't exist. The reading of a poem was an exercise in theory, to a certain extent, but it was also an exercise in feeling, and that was never, never played down at the University of Chicago. We were Tolstoyans, in that sense: we believed that the work of art was an expression of feeling that was supposed to induce a feelingful response in the reader. That was the whole purpose of it. And no matter how much you theorized, it was still the feeling that you were trying to get at.

What I saw happening later on in the seventies and eighties, the very rigorous and exclusive criticism that developed around European influences like Derrida and Lacan, I did not care for, and I still don't. At Chicago, we didn't have that. We were humanists, but in the good sense, not the narrow.

Contention did go on between the Artistotelians at Chicago and the New Critics at Kenyon and Indiana and Princeton. In fact, there was a lot of contention in the critical writing of that period. I had a tremendous admiration and liking for Yvor Winters, who lived out in California and was contending with everybody fiercely and vigorously all the time. I didn't agree with his opinions, mostly, but I liked the way he expressed them. Still, I found that the most useful criticism was not the contentious kind. A lot of very good *positive* criticism was being written in those days by people like Ransom. I remember one of the essays that had the biggest influence on me, not for what it said but for the way that it went about saying it: Randall Jarrell's essay on Robert Frost. It was a revelation, because most of the avant-garde writers thought that Frost was a nobody. Jarrell read Frost intelligently and critically but in a new way, a very sympathetic way, and brought him back into the colloquium, so to speak.

I was influenced by the essays of Eliot. I was influenced by the criticism of John Dewey, who was the complete opposite of Eliot. I was influenced by Kenneth Burke, whom I regard as one of the most important critics of that period, and different from the other New Critics. I used to read the magazines—*Partisan Review, Kenyon Review*, and so on—and was influenced by the people who wrote for them.

I always felt that critical writing *by poets* was probably

more important than critical writing by people who were *not* poets. The most important statements about poetry have been made, over the centuries, by working poets. I think it is important to have the experience of making your own poetry and knowing what goes into the imaginative process.

I never felt that criticism was evil or counterproductive, as some do. I always felt that criticism was intelligent, relatively. The human mind—whether one likes it or not—is a questioning organ. It wants to make inquiries, it wants answers, and it necessarily performs tasks of analysis and speculation and conjecture. And that's what criticism is—good criticism, anyway.

Like criticism, poetry can also perform tasks of analysis and speculation and conjecture. I've always felt that the aim of poetry and philosophy is the same: an understanding of the human situation. The poet approaches it imaginatively, the philosopher rationally. Those are the tendencies. Most poets are also rational, and most philosophers are also imaginative, but those are the tendencies. I don't see any incompatibility between them. I've always been interested in philosophy; I've always read quite a lot of it. And I've stuck it into my poems whenever I felt like it. But criticism falls somewhere in between philosophy and poetry. It asks questions about the relevance of the imagination to life and the relevance of poetry to the great metaphysical issues.

As a poet, I don't have to answer to myself as a critic. I don't avoid it; it just doesn't happen. When you're writing a poem, you're involved in the poem and, generally speaking, you don't think about issues of criticism. Although if you look at a poem you have written, and you see some kind of glaring stupidity in it, you'll take that out or throw the poem away. That's part of writing.

If you're working on a "big" poem, a poem that has to be programmatic, you may, to some extent, be guided by critical precepts. But in my case, my big poems, even though they're quite long, are composed of individual sections that have been written almost the same way I would write a small poem—and quite spontaneously.

As a graduate student, I was required to perform neo-Aristotelian analysis—to pay very concentrated attention to the text itself, how it was organized, how the rhetorical aspects were developed, and things like that. But at the same time, I learned a lot of history when I was at Chicago.

One of the things I had to do, since I had not been an English major earlier, was to take a survey course, which I think was intended primarily for upper-level undergraduates, and was taught by a fellow named Bond. His wife, Judith, was curator of the Modern Poetry Room in the library. I got to know both of them, and both were important to me. Bond's survey course was a very intense historical survey of all of English literature from the Middle Ages on. We read thousands and thousands of pages, and he gave very concentrated lectures. It was a big course; three or four hundred people were enrolled. That course was probably the most important I ever took, because I believe in history. I believe you have to know what went on in the past in order to understand what's happening in the present, and how one way of writing evolved out of another, and what the relationships are between writing and philosophy and painting and politics.

I was just coming to know the canon; I was making it up as I went along. I was reading a lot. I believed, and I still believe, that certain poets are better than other poets. I don't see how you can avoid that. A canon naturally results. Yours may not be the same canon as everybody else's, but that's a matter of consensus. The canon changes, and it should change. Often it changes radically.

That was one of the things we were taught at Chicago. We were often referred to Eliot's essay, "Tradition and the Individual Talent," about how the tradition changes from generation to generation because each one has its own insights and its own uses for the past. I was impressed by that idea, and I still am; I think it's right. The canon changes, but I think there is a canon, inevitably, and I don't think it is a bad thing. It brings us together and gives us a base of sensibility. I don't think of the canon as a rigid expression of taste. It's a broad expression of taste. It's an expression of *everybody's* taste. For me, the canon included people who were quite various, quite diverse—a lot of different strands.

My teachers were scholars. I had a tremendous admiration for them. There were still a few of the old-timers around when I was at Chicago; one of them was J. M. Manly. Back in the thirties, he and Edith Rickert had produced the variorum edition of *The Canterbury Tales* at Chicago, a huge and momentous scholarly undertaking. They had to collate all the manuscripts and do a lot of imaginative reading and guessing and emending. Old Manly was in his nineties, and he had an office. He didn't teach anymore, but he had an office up in the top of the library.

I often thought that if I had been different, if I had been somebody else, I would have liked to be a scholar like Manly. He was devoted. He was selfless. He had a tremendously learned headful of extraordinary information.

I've known scholars who were also fine poets. But in a lot of cases, I think, scholarship damages. I'm very grateful that I was later forced by the circumstances of my life to go and live on the Canadian frontier and do all the things I had to do to get along.

The place of a writer at any university is a difficult place, more so now than in recent years. I think many of the young poets who graduate with M.F.A.'s and then go out and get teaching jobs are limiting themselves terribly, though in some cases it may work out. I didn't begin to teach, myself, until I was almost sixty. I have never considered myself a real teacher, and I'm retiring at the end of this semester. So my relationship to the academy has been somewhat limited. But I tend to dislike the academicizing of literature and of writing.

We had no writers' workshops at Chicago when I was there; we had no training in writing at all, as I can recall. We were sometimes graded on how well we could write a critical essay, but I don't think I was ever taught how to do it. We studied literature, we studied theory, and we studied philosophy.

I think it's a mistake that writing has been turned into an academic discipline. There are a lot of other things writers can study at school that will do them more good than sitting around in a workshop and talking about the structure of a poem. You can say everything there is to be said about the structure of a poem in about twenty-five minutes.

A writer needs as big and general an education as he can get. I don't know as much about science as I wish I did. I would certainly recommend that writers *not* concentrate their formal schooling on literary studies. It's a good idea to know as much as you can about history and politics and science and philosophy and the other arts. And I think it's also necessary *not* to go to school all the time, but to get out in the world and find some kind of useful experience there. In leaving the university, I found myself, as a poet.

At Chicago I had a carrel in the library. I spent a lot of time there, and I spent a lot of time in the Modern Poetry Room up in one of the towers of the old library. Judith Bond's collection of poetry in the Modern Poetry Room had originally come from *Poetry* magazine. It was donated to the university by Harriet Monroe, *Poetry*'s founding editor, when she died, and consisted primarily of all the review books that had been submitted to the magazine over the years. So there was a lot of contemporary poetry, a lot of poetry that was minor and has been forgotten. I just poked around in that stuff and read as many different things as I could.

My own receptiveness is quite broad. I think that's why I became an editor. I've always been that way, interested in what other people were doing. I've done a lot of editorial work, and I'm receptive to other kinds of writing than my own.

Most writers are not very good editors. In order to be a good editor, you have to be able, somehow, to forget your own tastes, and any kind of prescriptive feeling you may have about writing, and open yourself up to what other people are doing. Like a good critic, you have to be able to put yourself inside the work that you're examining, and see if it meets its own ends, not *your* ends. A lot of writers can't do that.

I have always been fascinated by publishing and printing. One of the things I had done as a boy was to print. My father gave me a printing press and a couple of cases of type, and I used to set type and print little booklets and leaflets and dance tickets. Later I had a small press called the Crow's Mark Press.

In 1951 I became an editor at the University of Chicago Press—by accident. I was out of a job and looking for work; I wasn't having much luck. (I remember going over to the stockyards and trying to get a job as a publicity writer for Armour.) The Press gave me a job writing advertising copy for book jackets, catalog copy, and that sort of thing, for about 67 cents an hour.

I had worked there for less than a year when there was an upset in the management of the Press. The director was fired, and the associate editor went with him, as a matter of loyalty. And they asked me if I would take over the associate editorship. So I did, and became very involved in it.

Editing can become burdensome at times, because there's so much to do. I did an awful lot of work at the University of Chicago Press. In those days, we had only two associate editors; one was in science, and the other was in the humanities and social sciences. I was the humanities and social sciences editor, and at any given time I had something like four hundred books in various stages of development. So I worked very hard, took home a big briefcase every weekend, and that sort of thing. But I liked talking to the scholars, liked reading their manuscripts, liked working with them. One of the most interesting things I did was to work on the publications of the Oriental Institute. I loved those guys; they were true scholars. In those days, we didn't publish any poetry. We didn't publish any imaginative work at all. It was all scholarship.

In 1949–50 I was editor of *Poetry* magazine. In years past, Harriet Monroe had run the magazine by leaning financially on her North Side socialite friends. She was able to inspire them with a certain enthusiasm, but not much knowledge or sensitivity. So the Modern Poetry Association, the organization behind the magazine, had a lot of people in it who were not truly serious and didn't understand, for one thing, what I was trying to do as editor— which was why I eventually left. At the same time, though, good people were associated with the magazine—sincere and honest and intelligent people who did lend their support. People like Henry Rago, for instance, who did an excellent job as editor of the magazine for many years, were supported fully.

Rago was a poet and a teacher at the university who became editor of the magazine in 1955. He and I were very close friends. While still a Chicago student, I had been fortunate enough to get a couple of poems published in *Poetry;* George Dillon was the editor then. A number of people on his staff were very helpful and likable—John Nims, for one.

My problem when I was *Poetry*'s editor was that we were broke. After the war, in the late 1940s, there was tremendous inflation; the cost of paper and printing skyrocketed, and we had *no* institutional support. All we had were the contributions of the people who belonged to the Modern Poetry Association. So mostly what I did when I was there was try to raise money.

In those days, foundations would not even think of

giving money to a magazine. They wouldn't think of giving money to anything that they couldn't control. If a magazine goes to a foundation and says, we want you to support our publication during the next three years, the supporters can have no idea what's going to appear in that magazine during those three years. And in those days, what with the activities of the McCarthy Committee and the House Un-American Affairs Committee, potential donors were desperately afraid that if they gave money to *Poetry*, we would end up publishing a poem by a Communist, and we would be investigated, and *they* would be investigated. (I saw that actually happen later on when I worked at the Ford Foundation in New York.)

So it was hard to get money. Eventually, I did; I got a grant of a hundred thousand dollars from the Bollingen Foundation, which no longer exists. The grant saved the magazine. It was a lot, in those days, and it kept *Poetry* going for three years. (Ever since then, the magazine has been dependent on some kind of foundation support.)

I remember going to Bob Hutchins, at one point, and saying to him, "Look—the University of Chicago and *Poetry* magazine are *the* two, or possibly two of the three, most important cultural institutions in the city. Why don't you print us? Why don't you let your print shop print *Poetry* magazine?"

Hutchins said, "No, we just can't. We don't have enough money." Later on, of course, the university did take over the printing of the magazine.

There were other problems for me at *Poetry*. There was a thorny issue surrounding the controversy over the awarding of the Bollingen Prize to Ezra Pound. I supported that prize. I not only supported Pound, I published a booklet called "The Case Against *The Saturday Review*," because *The Saturday Review* had attacked the Bollingen Prize and the fellows of the Library of Congress who awarded the prize.

Some members of the Modern Poetry Association supported me, but not enthusiastically. They thought that I had gone too far in supporting Ezra Pound, so when I presented them with a plan of development for the magazine, they rejected it. In effect, I was fired, although it was not quite so blatant.

I wanted to make the magazine somewhat bigger. I wanted to include more news and more stuff that would be useful to poets. I wanted to make *Poetry* more of a trade paper for poets. The association just didn't take to it.

Chicago was an interesting city to live in because, for one thing, it was so corrupt. The neighborhood bars—including those near the university, on 55th Street—were wonderful places; they all had illegal activities going on, and interesting people: bookmakers and horse players and jazz musicians and bums and a lot of errant scholars, people who couldn't make it in the university but nevertheless were interested in some kind of scholarly endeavor, and had a lot of things to say. A strange mixture of people.

I was very interested in jazz music from the time I first heard it, back in the early thirties, and I went to listen to the jazz musicians in Chicago. I became friends with some of them. If I had been somebody else, I might have preferred to be a jazz musician. In some ways, I've gotten more pleasure out of jazz than poetry.

Jazz—and the African-American sensibility—are extremely important to American culture of the twentieth century. Finally people are beginning to recognize it. Our great jazz musicians, from the 1920s on down, have contributed more than any writers, I think, to the culture at large.

I have never known writers who were as selfless as the jazz musicians I knew in Chicago. When we listened to records and talked about them, there was no personal element, no rivalry, no ambition, nothing like what you find almost everywhere in the literary world. That kind of seriousness, that kind of devotion, certainly influenced me. I liked it, I appreciated it, and I tried to do the same thing in literature. In my criticism I tried very hard to do it, because I don't believe that criticism should be simply an expression of personal opinions, partial judgments, and all that kind of thing. The critic and the reviewer have other obligations, to the reader and to literature in general, that take precedence over whatever one's personal feelings may be.

I knew that poetry was what I had to do. I never thought that I could be a musician. I was so tense and insecure in public that there was no possibility. But my private, personal feelings about music were always important to my poetry.

Yet the music I heard in Chicago affected the music of my poetry in ways that are difficult to demonstrate. Somebody else, who was not interested in jazz, could point to his poems and show the same effects that are in my poems, and he would say that they didn't have anything to do with jazz, while I would say that in mine they do. There's no technical crossover between jazz and poetry; there can't be. So it's a matter of texture, of mood, of tone, a certain kind of improvisational syntax.

If jazz and poetry have something in common that means something to me, it might be freedom.

Jazz is a music that depends upon contrasting rhythms between melodic and rhythmical elements. The beat, the meter, is quite prominent, and it's exact. It does not vary. So the sense of propulsion and syncopation and force that you get out of jazz comes from the way the instrumentalist places his notes, his line of melody, against those beats. And he hardly ever plays *on* the beat; he always plays *off* it. He arranges his accents, his emphases, his rests, in a very free and spontaneous way. Jazz has a lot to do with phrasing, with the way syntax runs against the basic meter.

In poetry, your beat is unheard, if you're writing blank verse, for instance, in iambic pentameter. Consequently, you can play with the stresses and accents with a good deal of freedom. That's what great poets have always done.

I've always tried to get the effect of spontaneity into my poetry—not only the effect of spontaneity, but the effect of improvisation. A poem usually comes to me as a fragment of language, with a certain tone and a certain rhythm attached, and then builds from there. Improvisation is the fundamental quality of the 20th century in all the arts, even though most of them are not impromptu.

Music was an intensely personal thing to me, something that was happening *inside* me. My literary influences were significant, but more public than my musical influences. Literary texts are shared by a great many people. Although I talked with people about music, music was not transferable into language. Talking could not express what I felt when I was performing music or listening to it intently.

My outbursts were always very private.

By the time I left Chicago, I was pretty sick of it. I was glad to move away. But not long after, I began to get nostalgic about the place. I wrote a novel about Chicago of that period called *Appendix A*.

I was nostalgic partly for the city's neighborhood life. (I had lived in Hyde Park and in Woodlawn—close-knit, interesting communities.) Partly I just missed my friends, both at the university and up on the North Side and the Near North Side. I had known a lot of writers and artists there, and those were good people.

After I left the university, I went through a bad period of mental illness, and had to live in isolation. I wound up in the northern part of Vermont, working as a country laborer and doing hack work—book reviews, and stuff like that—to support myself. And I found my ways of writing and my topics primarily then, at that place and time. That was in the sixties.

I lived a very reclusive life for quite a long time. I *had* to develop my own resources, and I had to find out about myself. I had already been through a lot of psychotherapy, and that had helped. But mostly it was just being totally on my own—discovering that I *could* do that, that it was legitimate not to be an imitator of somebody else but to try to work on my own language, my own themes.

When I lived in Vermont, I did my writing in a little cabin surrounded by woods and fields. Frequently I worked at night, because I needed the daylight to do my outside work. And I would often hear the cry of a mouse being caught by an owl, or a rabbit being caught, being killed in the night.

Robert Coover

by Molly McQuade

Robert Coover earned an M.A. from the University of Chicago in 1965.

His books include the novels *The Origin of the Brunists* (Putnam, 1966), *The Public Burning* (Viking, 1977), *Whatever Happened
to Gloomy Gus of the Chicago Bears?* (Linden Press, 1987), and *Pinoc-
chio in Venice* (Linden, 1991), as well as the short-fiction collection
Pricksongs and Descants (Dutton, 1969). He teaches at Brown University.

Irony and precision of expression are part of a conversation
with Coover. He makes his points assertively. He is in earnest, in
pursuit. And though cerebral, Coover seems to give cerebral matters
a rather visceral quality. His independence means, one suspects, that
he would rather not be described by someone else.

ROBERT COOVER *Disturbing the dogmas*

Q: As a writer, you're known for your powers of invention, for breaking with literary tradition. But Chicago is quite a traditional school. What sort of link or disjunction was there between your education and your writing?

A: I came to Chicago after an undergraduate degree and nearly four years in the navy. I'd traveled a lot, read a lot, had my transformational encounter with Beckett's writing—the general experimental direction my writing was to take had probably already been formed. Good thing, too, because the prevailing mood at Chicago, I felt, was toward traditional orthodoxy. Not much room for formal experiment. But it didn't matter. I came to Chicago, really, to do a lot of reading in an organized way. I'd been somewhat adrift as an undergraduate, wandering unguided through the various disciplines, and my reading since then, though continuous, had been scattershot and uneven, in the typical way of the self-taught. What I wanted now was something traditional and hardheaded. I wanted to be provoked and tested. I got my wish. I signed up my first semester for a course with Richard McKeon.

It was a part of his year-long "Ideas and Methods" sequence, moving through the physical sciences, the social sciences, and the humanities. I arrived in the second term and started in the middle, and ended up in the sciences, which I'd always resisted but now found myself reading in a completely new and engaging way. Just the subtitles of the seminars, at least as I remember them, were, for an ill-read provincial like myself, an irresistible excitement:

"Motion, Time, Space, and Cause," "Freedom, History, and Power," and "Imitation, Imagination, Expression." It was like an open sesame into the whole world, or anyway that was the aura of it all.

Q: How did you read science in a different way?

A: As shifting discourse, instead of as an accrued body of knowledge. I began to understand, for example, that Einstein might be not so much an advance upon Newton as representative of a shift in modes of discourse, a change of philosophical fashion, so to speak. Obviously, there are accretions of a kind of knowledge that make some conclusions outdated, but the procedures by which you originally arrived at these outmoded conclusions could be adjusted to accommodate the new data without losing their validity as elemental forms of argument or dialogue. In the end, this played into my fiction writing, and helped me to understand "the death of the novel," as it's been called, and the imminence of fundamental formal changes.

At the heart of the McKeon system, which I think he called historical semantics, was a magical three-by-four matrix, within which we were invited to fit the entire history of rational human discourse. He was a classicist, of course, and claimed to have "discovered" this matrix in his studies of the ancient Greek philosophers, who therefore played a central role in all our gatherings, in or out of the classroom. Oddly, seen through the prism of his schema, the texts we studied seemed to lose their status as primary sources, and became instead the subject of another subject.

Personally, since I tended to be blinded by awe when confronted head-on by these heavy thinkers, this deflected gaze helped me a lot, though I can see how a pro in the field might be disturbed by it. The philosophy faculty generally, so far as I could tell, had little patience with McKeon's approach, which, because it roamed the disciplines so, could easily, on top of a fall from departmental grace, add a few extra years to the student's graduate studies. The department demanded a certain professionalization, as you might call it—you had to stay on track, complete a particular canonical reading, get through prelims, learn to talk the professional tongue, and McKeon disturbed all that. Certainly it put me at odds with the rest of the philosophy and history and English departments, and I often felt quite embattled in the more traditional courses. Of course, if you're cocky enough, that's fun, too.

Consequently, along with those few brave philosophers who bucked the conventional wisdom, McKeon's courses tended to fill up with people from all sorts of other disciplines—from law, from business, from theology and science, and of course from all those famous interdisciplinary committees that he himself had a lot to do with. He provoked a lot of very intense out-of-class exchanges. We recorded his lectures and the seminar discussions and then met every week on our own to listen to them, transcribe them, argue about them. These meetings would go on for hours, whether in someone's living room or in cellar quarters like my own or in a bar or down in the basement of Swift. He generated a charged intellectual atmosphere, the likes of which I had never seen before, nor have I since. I have since learned that we were not unique, that other generations of McKeon students have done exactly the same, gathering in impassioned debate over taped McKeon lecture playbacks, a venerable Chicago tradition perhaps not widely acknowledged.

Q: In the dedication to McKeon of your first novel, *The Origin of the Brunists,* you wrote, "See that you make them after the pattern for them, which has been shown you on the mountain." What did you mean by that?

A: That novel is about a religious cult that forms up around the survivor of a coal-mine disaster, and so uses a lot of biblical quotes. That one's meant, I think, as an acknowledgment of the revelatory impact McKeon had had on me at that formative moment, and the demanding standards he had set for me, which I tried to live up to in the researching and writing of the book. Also, I was able to read Christian history and theology with a more understanding eye and so avoid mere parody, even though I found the beliefs behind their traditional arguments pretty bizarre, and I'd been encouraged directly in this by McKeon, who'd agreed with me in principle but helped me to see any subject from a plurality of internally consistent philosophical positions. In that way, too, along with his magic matrix, he contributed to my development of characters, to a focus on significant action, to the patterns of the book.

It was at Chicago where, intellectually anyway, I finally came all the way into the world, and McKeon was at the center of that experience. I took one or two courses with him every term I was there, and all the rest of my course work circled around the reading I was doing with him, wide as the orbits might have been. He was controversial, too, of course, and that made him even more interesting. As humanities dean during the innovative Hutchins era, he had considerable influence on education at Chicago, but by the time I got there he had been shunted off into a dark corner of the Classics building and was pretty isolated, except for his students and a professorial acolyte or two, and, since our general opinion of the university at that time under Chancellor Kimpton was that it was passing through one of its most deadbeat purblind eras, he appeared to us as something of a hero out of the Golden Age.

What was happening at the university, of course, was only a reflection of what was happening everywhere else in those days. This was the tag end of the McCarthy era, you'll remember, the dull, narrow-minded Cold War days of the decaying Eisenhower presidency, with sputnik circling around up there, reminding everyone of the failures of the American educational system. So there was a lot of retrenchment going on. The disciplines were pretty isolated from one another, which made McKeon's method, with its ability to open windows onto every other field of knowledge, very appealing to many of us. It excited us to be able to talk about systems of law and government, medical practices, and theories of art, all in the same breath, and it sent us off reading in a thousand different directions at once, which I was inclined to do anyway. It was just made for me.

As was the Committee on General Studies in the Humanities, which I had chosen for my graduate studies because of the opportunity it offered to study in six different disciplines. Even so, I soon found even that too limiting and, much to the dismay of our committee chairman Norman Maclean, started signing up for courses in the theology, law, and Spanish departments before he stopped me.

Q: What did you think of Maclean?

A: When he wasn't playing General Motors junior executive, as he himself liked to put it, and I wasn't testing his patience with what he saw as a frivolous attitude toward the degree he was offering me and helping to pay for, we got on very well. He was crusty, warmhearted, supportive, often rather abrupt and testy. We called him "General Custer." He gave great barbecues every spring down at Pulaski Woods West, an event not to be missed. I took one Shakespeare course from him, which I did not find tremendously insightful. Blew an A in it, in fact, when on the final *King Lear* exam I decided to do a blatant parody of his own "Episode, Scene, Speech, and Word" essay, bringing his zoom-lens approach to bear on "Pillicock Hill," a kind of passing dirty joke. He didn't take to it kindly.

Q: He has been described as having certain fundamental conflicts—as being in conflict over his Westernness, for example, and over the sort of romantic image of it which he himself projected. He has also been described as being someone who was not really introspective, so that he had to find other ways of getting around the conflicts.

A: Older persons, peers of his who knew him better, would probably have a fuller sense of him than I could have. I was his student, he was my adviser, obviously our relationship was more formal and distant, in spite of his blunt, head-on way of talking to people. It was my impression, though, that he *was* an introspective man. There was always a lot of silence around him, long moments when he seemed to be chewing on his thoughts, so to speak, mulling things over. Those tough, crusty remarks of his, when he did get them out, had a kind of practiced quality, as though he'd worked them out before he spoke them.

We had one pretty bad moment when I wrote him a rather presumptuous letter, criticizing his shopkeeping mentality as a committee chairman. I was living at the time on the GI Bill, scholarships, and editing jobs, including that of the university's Weekly Calendar. He took away the scholarship. But then he gave it back again. We got on well after that, and even better after he retired.

I didn't know he was writing fiction while I was there, but I guessed it from our conversations. He would ask, out of the blue, about Hemingway, for example, provoking me into an argument about style, much as writer friends of mine would do, and we soon guessed that he was working out his own stylistic or other problems with these conversations, which often began and ended quite abruptly. So when, after his retirement many years later, his first book came out, I wasn't too surprised. *A River Runs Through It* is a terrific piece of writing, formally remote from my own narrative preferences, but I like it very much.

I don't think he was a great academic thinker, though, and I got the feeling he did not feel very happy about being around a lot of academics. They did not appeal to him as people. He wasn't up to the best of them in terms of intellect and scholarly endeavor, and they knew this, and he knew they knew. It had to cause a certain estrangement. He was linked to the Chicago School by circumstance more than by his writing, but he was never really a part of that gang and probably always felt a bit out of place around them, which would have made him seem more conflicted, more brusque, and less, as we would say, introspective.

Q: What did *you* think of the Chicago School?

A: I was so remote from criticism in general that it took me a long time actually to realize that it existed. When people talked about the Chicago School, I thought they were talking about the university high school or something. Finally, when I was reading everything I could find that McKeon had written, I came on *Critics and Criticism* and got engaged with it. I read it through the lens of the McKeon schema, of course, and found great intellectual rapport between McKeon and R. S. Crane, with Elder Olson tagging along behind; but in retrospect, I think, like most so-called schools, the Chicago School really wasn't one, except in so far as, following McKeon, it championed discourse on the nature of discourse and favored what might be called a kind of dialectical pluralism.

Q: Did the university affect your writing in other ways?

A: Sure. Got a lot out of just wandering the stacks, my pass and desk there more for the writing than for the course work. Picked up a bit of Gothic atmosphere, walking through the quad on foggy winter evenings. When I felt oppressed by overdue papers or looming exams, I often sat in the Swift Hall basement, sipping coffee and scribbling out notes for stories or revising old ones.

Elder Olson's prosody and theory of lyric poetry and modern theater courses were all valuable, other drama courses, too: a lot of ritual and spectacle in the *Brunists* and everything else I've done I was chasing at Chicago. There was also a congenial old historian named Cate, who emphasized for me the importance of detail, and an eloquent hunchbacked art historian named Blanckenhagen, a former Nazi, we were told, who waxed so passionate one day on the ideal beauty of the Classic Greek form that he fell off the little stage, then clambered right back up without losing a beat in his praise of the sublime, an image that's carried me through a lot of pratfalls of my own.

But the greatest stimulus to writing at a place like Chicago, I suppose, is not the university itself but everything happening at the edges. The conversations in Jimmy's or sitting out on the grass or over barbecue at Gordon's, the bookstore browsing, the music, the film clubs, theater, on campus and off. Improvisational theater, the kind that was making Chicago famous, was just starting up while I was there, and there were poetry and prose readings, with people like Frost and Eliot and e. e. cummings coming through—including an extraordinary and courageous reading by Flannery O'Connor of "A Good Man Is Hard to Find" one night in an empty Mandel Hall that has remained a standard for me through all the ups and downs of my own public readings ever since. I took courses down at the Art Institute, imagining a whole other life. And there were a lot of writers hanging around, not all students, meeting in bars or at readings or in the *Chicago Review* office or in soiree fashion in improvised workshops. There was always a feeling that something was happening and you were in the middle of it, and that, plus a good library, is probably all any writer needs. And some good bookstores—plenty of those in the neighborhood back then. I loaded up on books. The real starting point of whatever library I have was there.

Q: Philip Roth has written about the same thing—how he would allow himself to buy a certain number of books every week, and gradually accumulate a library. Did you meet him while you were there?

A: No, he left a few months before I arrived, though I was a good friend of one of his former roommates, and met many people who'd known him. He was known around campus as a very funny man. And of course his book *Goodbye, Columbus* came out while I was there and was read avidly and enviously by all the Hyde Park writers.

Q: Roth recalled one of Richard Stern's classes in which Saul Bellow was invited to discuss a student's story. As it happened, Roth's story, "The Conversion of the Jews," was discussed.

A: Bellow became a big supporter of the book, too, when it came out. So, such links are made. I applied for one of Dick's workshops while I was there, offering up one of my little breakaway fictions as a writing sample, but he rejected me. Quite rightly, too, I would have done the same.

Stern has always been generously supportive of other writers, and did eventually introduce me to Bellow, though that was years later, when I finally returned to hand in my M.A. thesis. I was about to tear up the first draft of *The Origin of the Brunists* and start over, and the very reason I was writing that book, which at the time was causing me a lot of frustration, had had something to do with Bellow. While I was still a student at Chicago, some years before, Bellow had started up a new literary magazine, *The Noble Savage,* along with a couple of colleagues at Bard College, where he was teaching. I read the first issue, sensed a pattern in what they'd published, rewrote an old coal-mining story from my undergraduate days, and sent it off. They accepted it for the fourth issue, my first fiction acceptance. I immediately sent them some of my more recent experimental fictions, ones that appeared later in *Pricksongs and Descants,* but Bellow and the others found them "sensationalist" and lacking in "the *human* content of art," suggesting that I should maybe bury them in a bottom drawer somewhere. After the story appeared, I got the same response from New York editors, who found my more innovative writing unpalatable and asked me if I didn't have something "a bit more like the story that Bellow published in *The Noble Savage?*" So I began to invent one, just to have some sort of reply, and that was how *The Origin of the Brunists* was born.

Q: You've mentioned the *Chicago Review,* which, as you

probably know, continues to be more interested in experimental fiction than in realism. Was that true at the time?

A: Actually, there were two times, the Irving Rosenthal era of Beat mania, when the staff fell under what the faculty felt to be the demonic influence of the poet Paul Carroll, and the more conservative Pak era that followed—before and after the famous blowup, that is, that created *Big Table* magazine.

Q: What's your view of that blowup?

A: Well, it was a clear case of literary suppression, of book banning. I *said* it was a dismal era at the university as far as the administration went. The student editors were enamored of the Beats and were ready to publish *everything,* including "wish-you-were-here" postcards from Beat travels abroad, and to the exclusion of just about every other kind of writing. Nothing wrong with that, of course—excess is one of the great virtues of a student-run magazine. No chance it will be long-lived, because student generations so quickly come and go. You just live and prosper or sometimes suffer with the shifting enthusiasms.

But writers like Burroughs and Kerouac were full of four-letter words, and the city's yellow journalists had been raising the old "filth and obscenity" alarm, which in turn had got the trustees riled up, so there was a lot of pressure from the top down to suppress the next issue, also, of course, dedicated to more of the same. I wasn't privy to the various negotiations and ultimatums, but as I understood it at the time, there were people like the chancellor who wanted to see the *Review* itself dead and buried once and for all, others who only wanted to suppress that particular issue, these being supposedly the liberals, and, finally, in this context, there were the faculty advisers like Dick Stern who wanted the editors to hold the accepted Beat material for at least one issue and do another first that was more balanced. All of which represented a faint-hearted knuckling under to the yahoos. The reaction of the editors was to resign en masse, all except Pak, and to create *Big Table*, a legendary moment in Chicago's literary history.

Q: Stern said he himself was published in *Big Table*.

A: Yes? Well, I'd forgotten that, but I'm not surprised. It was my impression at the time that the *Review* editors had anticipated and even planned for the administration's reaction. I think they wanted the notoriety of it. Scandal made a nice send-off for the new magazine. If I remember rightly, one of the writers published even dedicated his story to the book banners for helping to launch the new magazine. And it was, during its short life, a lively publication. It made a big splash around town and around the country.

Its editor was Paul Carroll, and his role in the *Chicago Review* story is still something of a mystery to me. He was a poetry adviser or editor under Rosenthal, but was not associated in any way with the university at that time, so far as I know, so I don't know what he was doing on the staff. It was widely assumed that he was largely responsible for the naughty direction the magazine had taken, but I don't recall any official complaints about his presence there from the administration.

Pak, who took over, was rather academic, but a good editor who produced a decent, serious literary magazine. He read carefully, tended shop dutifully, and watched over the magazine in a cool, professional way. But I believe the whole thing should never have happened. The faculty directive was a big mistake. What a board like that should do is see that the magazine gets the money it needs and see that the money it has is not overspent—be sure that someone's in the shop, that is, and the magazine is actually being managed. Other than that, they should keep their hands off, let what happens happen, and defend the student staff vigorously against the louts and the Bowdlers.

Q: Many writers who went to Chicago also teach. How

did you end up teaching, and when you teach do you have in mind teachers you had at Chicago?

A: By necessity, to answer the first part of your question. We lived on the writing as long as and whenever we could, but finally it wasn't enough to keep the family fed. I have to admit I like teaching, like the dialogue, the seminar situation, but it absorbs me entirely and I find I don't write at all when I teach, so I feel it's a mistake—even, given my feelings about this vocation, immoral. And yet I don't know how I would have got through these last years without it.

But as to the second part of the question, which is more interesting, I suppose that in some respect I have felt the need to reshape the curriculum all the time, and this is something that McKeon always did, and it was also characteristic of all the special interdisciplinary committees at Chicago. One of the limitations of the typical university program is that the disciplines isolate themselves from one another, and then establish a canon and create a somewhat arbitrary sense of what it means to be a professional in that discipline, exclusive of all others. I like to break into that isolation whenever I can, disrupt the norm, disturb the dogmas; and I encourage my writing students to try to do the same by way of the courses they take.

I hope I don't imitate McKeon in style, though, because his classroom manner could be pretty intimidating. On principle, he favored the Socratic method, but he always had a very clear agenda for the day, so his attempts at seminar dialogue were usually pretty short-lived. And he had a way of hitting you with some absolutely awesome and unanswerable question before you could even get started.

I remember the first course I took from him, the first class meeting. We'd been assigned a number of pages of Spinoza to read, and I'd gone over them a thousand times, first day in graduate school and all that. I thought I was pretty well prepared. He came into the room, took out his class list and notebook, tucked his pipe in his mouth, and, running his finger down the class list, asked, "Mr. Coover, what does Spinoza have to say about God?" About God? I couldn't remember a single mention of God in the entire text. The only thing I felt was that I'd just been fingered by Him. I mumbled some hapless idiocy, McKeon snorted in disgust, went to another name on his list. My only consolation was that at least a dozen others suffered exactly the same fate, and others simply weren't answering when he called their names, ducking and pretending not to be there.

Finally, he called on a long wiry string bean of a fellow, a philosophy major, as I later learned, who had the peculiar nervous habit of bugging his eyes out and rocking stiffly back and forth in his chair when he spoke. That's what he did now: raised his eyebrows and started to rock. We were all mesmerized, watching him. McKeon, too, maybe. Finally he said, "Well [*rock rock*], I notice that the section [*rock rock*] is divided into two parts—" "*Right!*" exclaimed McKeon, cutting him off, and he got up and proceeded to lecture us. Actually, it was a very important lesson. Two parts. I never forgot it.

Q: Any regrets?

A: Yes. I loved the University of Chicago. I think I had to leave too soon. I would have been glad to stay around longer.

Leon Forrest

Leon Forrest, a lifelong Chicagoan, studied at the University of Chicago from 1958 to 1960 and again from 1963 to 1964.

He is a novelist and a playwright who has also worked as a journalist and an editor and has taught at Yale University, Wesleyan, and elsewhere. Forrest is now chair of the African-American Studies Department at Northwestern University.

His novels include *There Is a Tree More Ancient Than Eden* (Random House, 1973), *The Bloodworth Orphans* (Random, 1977), *Two Wings to Veil My Face* (Random, 1983), and *Divine Days* (Another Chicago Press, 1992).

Forrest is nothing if not genial. His sweetness seemed tempered yet not sharpened by difficulty as he remembered the struggle both to become a writer *and* to do the writing.

LEON FORREST *The yeast of chaos*

For a writer, the ideal artistic community is made up of musicians, painters, a few writers—and a lot of people interested in the arts in a general way. I was drawn to the University of Chicago because I thought I would find that community there.

I lived in a building at 61st and Dorchester, right across from the university. Musicians and painters and writers lived in it with me. It was owned by an elderly Jewish woman who had been a Communist, though not a card-carrying one. She had all these wonderful records of Paul Robeson's. In the building there were a lot of political people and people of different races—Africans, Indians. I was hanging out, hanging around, meeting a wonderful group of people.

At the same time, I was trying to write. I was also working for a community newspaper and later for the Muslim paper *Muhammad Speaks.* I was teaching a creative writing class at Kennedy-King Junior College one day a week. I was taking classes at the University of Chicago.

That was a time of great chaos in my life, because I was trying to find my way as a writer. I had a lot of energy. I heard all those different voices and saw all those different lives, and they all were struggling to achieve themselves. My problem was to *make* something out of this.

Chaos is very important to a writer—all of this life bubbling around, and you trying to get in there and take what you need from the material and then transform it into something.

You have to take what you can, then ultimately drift

away from it in order to shape what you need. But initially there must be chaos, so that you can place your stamp on it. You must be attracted to it and not let it destroy you. And that's really a fight. In a lot of cases, chaos destroys writers, either through the destructive nature of the writer, or through addiction to the scene itself—the frantic people who take over your life and waste you, or alcohol, or drugs, or just you, running the streets to your detriment and ultimately becoming more of a *talker* than a writer, a priest of the bars.

The things that I loved in life and wanted to convert and transform into literature were themselves filled with the yeast of chaos. I might have been destroyed by the chaos I was so drawn to that I couldn't get a hold on it. And I couldn't get a hold on my own sort of discipline, either. There was a tension between discipline and chaos. My battles were between the flesh and the spirit; they were about the question of race, about the question of how to write out of a sensibility of oppressed people, about the fact that so many heroes of that drama were people filled with rage and chaos who eventually lost their lives in the struggle. And my battle was intensified by the fact that, in wanting to become a writer, I was joining a minority within a minority. Models were few, Ellison being one.

In the Irish and the Jewish cultures, a writer, an intellectual, was admired. In the black culture, no. This contributed to my chaos. I couldn't seem to finish anything. I couldn't finish school. I couldn't finish anything. It was awful. I had to develop a certain sturdiness, and it was touch and go whether I ever would.

I ended up at the University of Chicago because of an ambition I had, fostered in me by my parents and by my teachers in grade school and in high school.

My father was a bartender on the railroad. We were lower-middle-class. He was a self-made man, hypersensitive and high-strung. So it was kind of difficult to get to him. I wasn't tough enough to speak up to him. Daddy was absolutely certain that I was going to become a doctor—based on nothing!

My family had a lot of great storytellers, mostly my aunts and uncles. And my father used to come back from his railroad job with stories. He was a very engaging man, so he'd bring stories from jazz musicians as well as from the whites on the train who would talk to him. Daddy would also read a lot to me, and so would my mother. Because I was the only child of two only children, I was the pet of the family. I'd sit around and listen to people talk, and I would *not* break into the conversations of adults. Maybe I wanted to, but maybe I had the good sense not to!

They would read anything to me that they could get their hands on. My father would take books out of the library and read to me—books by Zane Grey and so on. Until I was about nine, my great-grandmother lived with us, and I would read the Bible to her and with her. Later I was raised partly by a woman who lived with us all of my growing-up years. She was a spinster from Kentucky. She would read to me, and I would read to her. I also had the task after Mass of reading the Gospel and the Epistle to an invalid—an aunt on my mother's side, the Catholic side.

My father was interested in writing; he wrote songs and had two published. (He never made any money from them.) He had a very nice singing voice, kind of like an Irish tenor mixed in with the sound of the Ink Spots' Bill Kenney. He recorded some of his songs.

People often talk about a writer's voice. Quite early, I had a very physical sense of what it was. And the black singers I heard—Billie Holiday and Sarah Vaughn, and particularly Dinah Washington—had a lot of influence on my sense of the *art* of the voice, the voice's particular nuances.

So all this was brewing in me for a long time before I ever consciously wanted to write, but my problem always was to take that rich oral eloquence and try to do something with it. In making this transition, writers like Faulkner and Hardy and Ellison, all great storytellers, were very helpful to me.

I was drawn to the Bible as a connection, as a source. The Bible is an organic text in the life of blacks. The eloquence of the prophets in the Old Testament is recombined into a kind of literary resiliency.

In the Chicago of my youth, a wonderful range of Negro preaching was available. The art of the folk preacher has often provided my writing with a base. Aretha Franklin's father, C. L. Franklin, was one of America's tremendous preachers—his sermons were recorded, and I knew of them. They touched me with an oral, verbal immediacy, but also made some interesting stabs at an intellectual framework.

This is the thing: to move from that verbal emotion and ecstasy into a higher state of literary consciousness. The poems of Dylan Thomas and Yeats and particularly the sermons of John Donne brought occasions like marriage and death to a higher pitch, a more profound eloquence.

I'm Catholic on my mother's side. My mother's people are from Louisiana and my father's from Mississippi. It's through his family that I became aware of the gospel voice.

These two sides of my family—Mississippi on the one hand, Louisiana on the other—were both very much a part of the oral tradition and the oral education that I received.

What the writer learns outside of school is as important as what he or she learns inside it. I've always been overwhelmed by the bold blast of music out of Creole culture, the outrageousness of the New Orleans experience. It gave life to jazz, to honky-tonk, to cuisine. And it's produced some really outrageous and complex people, subtle with all kinds of shadings that have to do with the connections of French and Spanish and African character. The intergroup racism about color within that culture is heartbreaking, but at the same time, I greatly admired the energy of the culture.

Together, New Orleans and Mississippi represented a kind of mythical Old Country for me, as the South did for James Baldwin. Baldwin didn't grow up in the South; he was a New Yorker.

All my cousins on my mother's side went to Catholic school at a time when Catholics did very little to encourage learning about the richness of black culture. I went to the Wendell Phillips grade school, an all-black public school in Chicago. I later went on to a predominantly white high school and college. Wendell Phillips was helpful in securing my identity. But I always went to a Catholic church, and there I was very much impressed with the ritual.

Interest in ritual and myth carried over into my writing. But I got a much better grounding in racial sensibility from the Protestant side and from some wonderful black teachers at Wendell Phillips.

In some ways, we benefited at Phillips because of the *lack* of opportunities available to our teachers. We had all these wonderful women, and a few men, too, who threw their lives into their teaching. They were what we used to call race men and women. They provided a certain racial uplift—within segregation, but they were always grounding us in the tradition of new writers: Paul Laurence Dunbar, Langston Hughes, Richard Wright.

Hyde Park High School, which I attended afterward, was predominantly white. In educational quality it ranked about fifteenth in the country and second or third in the state. It was a magnet for upper-middle-class Jewish families and for a few black families. A lot of students were the children of University of Chicago faculty. We had some extraordinary teachers there, all white, who had taught for thirty or forty years.

I was at Hyde Park from 1951 to 1955. By the time I graduated, about two-thirds of the entering freshmen were black. So it was a time of transition. The transition from mostly white to mostly black happened very rapidly, and there was no attempt to do something for the average student or the mediocre student or the student who had little preparation. Meanwhile, a lot of the legendary teachers were either getting pretty old or had sort of lost interest. It was a wonderfully competitive environment, and it was great if *you* were competitive and ambitious, but otherwise you could get lost.

When I graduated, I went first of all to Woodrow Wilson Junior College, then to Roosevelt, and then to the University of Chicago. At the same time, my parents had divorced and my mother had remarried. She married a man who had a tavern, and I dropped out of college and started working there. Then I went into the army. When I came back, I re-enrolled at Chicago as a student at large. So I didn't take a degree, but I took a great many literature courses.

It's very important to the education of a writer that he or she find an intellectual mother or father. At Hyde Park High School, I had an extraordinary teacher, Mrs. Edith Thompson, who was interested in creative writing. I wanted to write poetry, and she was my mentor. She encouraged me; I became president of our creative writing class.

Then Mrs. Thompson was accused of running an abortion ring! Eventually the police rescinded this rap, and she was officially reinstated, but she never returned to teach. I went to the principal about it, and we students circulated a petition—but she didn't come back.

This brought out a couple of qualities in me that I hadn't known about. One was that I could become a fighter when somebody was mistreated. (When the crisis in Mrs. Thompson's life came along, I saw it as an attack on a mother figure.) Another was loyalty.

Later, Allison Davis was an intellectual father to me. He was a cultural anthropologist who taught in the University of Chicago's School of Education. His specialties were the gifted child and educational psychology. Davis was the first black to get tenure at a major northern university. I met him at International House about 1966, and we struck up a friendship that lasted many years. My first novel was dedicated to Allison. He had a strong influence on my thinking and writing. Though he was a scholar and not a novelist, he had broad literary interests that made him a valued intellectual colleague.

Another influence on my intellectual growth was a University of Chicago professor named Perrin Lowrey. Lowrey was an authority on Faulkner. He was also a writer and had published a collection of short stories. He was a Southerner, a Mississippian. I took creative writing classes with him.

Lowrey was an intellectual uncle to me. He introduced me to certain books and also to the idea that the writer must develop a critical intelligence. Previously, my writing had mainly been drawn from spiritual and emotional juices.

Through Lowrey I met a junior colleague of his, John Cawelti. Cawelti and I struck up an acquaintanceship that has flowered over the years. (In fact, Cawelti wrote the introduction to one of my recently reissued novels.) Another professor who influenced me was Marvin Mirsky, with whom I took many classes. Mirsky was one of the finest teachers I ever had—vastly well read, wonderfully analytical about literature.

I took a creative writing class from John Logan—a wonderful poet who had an extraordinary life. Naomi Lazard was one of the poets in the class, and others came out of it, too.

I met Marge Piercy through a writing group that met in Hyde Park. There were about thirty people in the group—all white except one or two; we would meet twice a month. I sort of floated in and out.

At the time, Piercy was writing poetry, not fiction. Of all of us, she had the best intellect. She was a good critic, intelligent, very well read. And she was involved with a friend of mine, a Southerner who was a writer. Like many others in the group, he was very talented but never published anything. This fellow even had a contract for a novel but never finished it. Subsequently, he drifted away. We also had a Trinidadian writer who was *so* talented, a wonderful storyteller. He had a large family back in Trinidad, and he got caught up in real estate. Another writer in the group, who published many novels, was Harry Mark Petrakis. I remember I was in class when Petrakis sold his first short story. He had been writing for years.

Figures like these are important in the life of a writer. They encourage you in times of crisis in your own life—crises in confidence or times when you are fumbling with this yeast of talent to convert it into something else. If intellectual fathering or mothering is going to work well, it must happen in a natural, uncalculated way. I stumbled into Mrs. Thompson—and certainly into Allison.

A writer needs three educations: to read a great deal; to listen a lot (that's oral tradition); and to learn the actual craft of writing, which comes through imitating very good writers. You're usually drawn to your own writing by being overwhelmed or fascinated by some other writer. Of course, you break away from imitation through rewriting and through the assertion of your will, your ego, your style, and your own material. To make such breakthroughs requires the kind of intellectual ability that is nurtured by a university.

To be a writer of substance, you have to be something of an intellectual, though not necessarily a scholar—hopefully not! Oh dear, sitting around, hovering over one play by Shakespeare all my life? No, not that. But there must be intellectual fire. Some of that was always there, for me, yet it was only smoldering, almost smothered by an avalanche of literary influences.

I've always been very much taken with the possibility of capturing a sensibility through language and transforming oral eloquence into literary eloquence. The writers who most influenced me were writers who were in the first instance poets. Thomas Hardy was one of the first, along with Edgar Allan Poe, and then in college Faulkner and James Joyce. Another was Dylan Thomas. For a long time, I also wanted to write plays, and felt attracted to certain writers—Eugene O'Neill and Tennessee Williams among them—who were *poets* of the theater. These writers overwhelmed me with the poetry of their art.

In the early seventies, I began to get interested in Russian literature. It was a real source. At the same time, I became quite interested in Latin American literature. The Latin American writers were wrestling with some of the same problems I was: how to take an essentially oral culture and transform it into a literary one; how to deal with the problem of slavery, the problem of belonging to an oppressed people. The bold and outrageous literature of García Márquez and José Donoso gave me boldness.

The black writers whom I admired, too—Robert Hayden and Ellison—were interested in much the same transformation. *Invisible Man* impressed me. It was Ellison's eloquence, and his great storytelling, that did it. These were the things I really hungered for in my fiction.

I had great problems with the black aesthetic, and shunned it. I saw the black arts movement as a dead end. For that reason, I didn't have a lot of contact with black writers—with the black *young* writers who were part of that movement.

I thought it was a segregationist movement, limited and limiting. I thought that it was racist and that it short-circuited the great richness of black life. I was very attracted to certain dimensions of race pride, but the movement was intellectually dead.

The Irish writers I most admired had handled nationalism with such cunning and depth. You need some of this; it's part of the rise of any people. But the narrowness of nationalism can cut you off from developing intellectually. You can get caught up in the worship of your culture to a point where it is parochial and pretentious. It can keep you from taking on the viable connections to world culture. It can keep you from being critical of your own culture. You need some of that nationalistic energy to foster a political movement and a cultural movement. But if you don't take that to the next step, which is a broadness and a flowering, it can be deadly. That's what I saw happening with the black aesthetic movement.

During my days as a University of Chicago student, a lot of black writers were trying to make art out of polemics, instead of transforming the polemics of the culture into art. I was working as a newspaperman while I was a student, and this gave me a way to deal directly with the visceral political issues of the day. That was very healthy, because it forced me, when I came home to write fiction, to try something else. When I came to my own fiction, I could work in the way of an artist, which is what I'd always wanted to do. I thought that *this* could be the most meaningful and moving contribution to my people and to myself—to develop my talent into an instrument that was artful and angular and layered and transformed. Multilayered. As complicated as African-Americans are. Irreducible.

Malcolm X to me represented this kind of angularity of character, what Dostoyevsky calls a soul struggle in terms of politics and religion: he was constantly, passionately in search of who he was. Whereas a lot of my polemical friends were bowled over by Malcolm as *knowing who he was*, I saw the man as divided, in chaos.

All these writers educated me and gave me confidence in using and shaping certain materials in my own culture. But when you're overwhelmed by someone or something, you do have to step back at some point. That's very true.

It's true in love. And I felt that way, certainly, with these writers and also with the great black entertainers who made such an impression on me: Mahalia Jackson, the great dancers, the wonderful singers, the tap dancers. All of them were overwhelming figures. So I've always had to try to move back from all that, to pick myself up.

How do I pick myself up? Well, it takes a long time to do it. Ultimately, of course, it's the life of the mind that makes you do it. One of the things I had to ferret out was how and why I was ultimately drawn to these people. You're drawn because you're nourished by these personalities; the meaning of life is revealed. But in the initial stages—the stages you pass through when you are young—it's the emotional fire that counts. And you may not understand, at first. Your need is too great.

As a young man, I was chaotic and romantic, like my father. I was always falling in and out of love, being overwhelmed by female beauty, and so on. And in a way, that's necessary. It's necessary that life overwhelm you, and you engage, and then out of that try to shape something. It's a struggle that's good.

Yet the older I've grown, the more fascinated I've become with the artists who've lived long lives. Maybe they have more wisdom. Maybe *they* have stepped back. The life of the mind—and a spiritual life—has had time to flower and flourish.

I'm less romantic now. I'm attracted to a certain lyricism and fire and magic, but, conversely, it's hard to achieve that *and* a certain kind of maturation, too. Romanticism must give way to other things, such as spiritual development. A certain combativeness is part of the romantic identity, a kind of foolishness in seeking perfection in love and in yourself and in others. When you are so devouring of other people, you don't allow *them* to flower, or yourself.

Obviously, as art takes over your life, you have to be more and more a kind of priest and live with your own solitude. To find that state of mind is very difficult. When you find it, you have to accept the fact that you're married to your art.

Though I'm less romantic now, I still love the romance of life. It's a very difficult thing to maintain, because of the crassness of the world. A lot of people take romance to the point of a kind of corruption of feeling. The life of an academic constantly shows up the absurdity in this.

The University of Chicago was, and still is, a place of high intellect and high art, and a place where one learns to appreciate one's solitude. It's all right to be a priest of solitude there.

June Jordan

June Jordan, a poet, a novelist, and a political essayist, is the author of *Things That I Do in the Dark* (Random House, 1977), *Passion* (Beacon Press, 1980), *Naming Our Destiny: New and Selected Poems* (Thunder's Mouth, 1989), and *Haruko/Love Poems* (High Risk/Serpent's Tail, 1993). In addition to those collections of poetry, she has published essay collections, among them *On Call: Political Essays* (South End Press, 1985) and *Technical Difficulties* (Pantheon, 1992). She attended the University of Chicago as an undergraduate beginning in 1955.

Interviewed in Berkeley, where she is a professor of African-American studies at the University of California, Jordan was forthright in sharing her thoughts and taking a strong stance on the purposes of education and its occasional drawbacks. She is an attentive listener, as well as a forceful and eloquent speaker.

JUNE JORDAN *Getting angry*

Chicago—the city and the university—is set up for the fittest. A ferocious kind of value system undergirds the whole thing: the fittest will survive, and the others will perish. And so it happens.

As a University of Chicago student, I knew I was an artist, not an academic kind of person. I always had the candid ambition to be a great poet. I never stopped writing poetry; I never gave up.

But I felt acutely uncomfortable about myself, situated, against my will, in an academic enclave that bordered on a low-income black neighborhood, from which I was separated by so many things. I was a newlywed woman, a very young woman, and I had never been to Chicago before. My husband Michael was white, and his parents lived in Hyde Park, a white neighborhood. It was mostly white except for me. I was the only nonwhite that I can remember in student housing. There were extremely few people of color at the university. On the South Side of Chicago, it seemed to me that white people and black people had nothing to do with each other; they were almost totally separated.

My in-laws were racist, actually, and they were upset that their son had married me.

So I was not living a blissful life.

My idea was that I should just persevere, humbly, in what I felt was my effort to be a great poet *as* a black woman. And just keep doing it. Just keep writing.

One of the things I felt and still feel is that poetry represents the most exacting use of language. Every other form of writing is a lesser undertaking. But at Chicago I ran into the essay form. And I felt that something in this form, though not commensurate with poetry, was also exacting.

I was an English major, and the professor for one of my courses was Stuart Tave. In Tave's class, we were studying the romantic essayists, meaning Carlyle, Charles Lamb, De Quincey, and Hazlitt.

Hazlitt I liked a lot. He was tremendous, exciting, politically clear, spirited, and wrote really well. Lamb was also interesting. Before reading him, it had not occurred to me that a man might think that way: he seemed enmeshed in the daily minutiae of mind. De Quincey was, I thought, an articulate drug addict. And I remember thinking, "Carlyle is a crackpot"; he thought he was God.

It was necessary to write a term paper for Tave's course, so I did. Everybody else got their papers back, but I didn't. Finally, when a couple of weeks had gone by, I asked, "Where's my paper?"

Tave called me into his office. He said, "Your writing is so . . ."—and though he didn't use the word "bizarre," that was the idea: bizarre and Byzantine—"that I thought I should put it in the cupboard and let it stay there for a while, and see if, when I took it out, it had become more decipherable." So he literally went to a cupboard, took out my paper, started rereading it, and said, "No, it's still impenetrable to a rational reader."

Now, I had taken courses in English at Barnard College. I knew I was a gifted writer. This was ridiculous! I went home and said to my husband, "Michael, I'm not going to stay at this school."

That was the first time in my life that I had ever written anything, prose or poetry, about which the teacher or reader had come back to me and said anything other than "Wow." Tave was adamant. He even asked me if English was my first language.

In those days, my attitude about the University of Chicago was mixed. I had already read essays by Robert Hutchins, because I had been interested in education per se, philosophically. I had been very excited by what he had to say, and I thought that what might be termed the Chicago experience was extremely important. I wish I had been old enough to have participated in the Hutchins experiment, and not come after it. But this *was* after it.

And now I had been evaluated as functionally illiterate by an English professor.

I didn't consider Tave racist, because in those days I didn't think in quite those terms. Yet I felt that the fact that I was not white and was a girl led him to disrespect me and to expect me not to do well. He probably just thought, What is she doing here? What is she doing at the University of Chicago? Which was indeed my question, as well!

When I arrived in Chicago, I was already aware of race discrimination, as I would have called it then, and had worked actively against it with the NAACP as a student in New York City. But other areas of political struggle were not known to me. In Chicago, some became clear to me—or clearer. I became aware of class and, in a very incipient way, gender at the university. I developed an inchoate sense of class, apart from race. For the first time, it occurred to me that it might be problematic to be an artist, period—as well as problematic for me as a black woman.

The university was overwhelmingly white, and the curriculum was strictly European. I wish that I could have learned, at the time, more about literatures than one. Western European literature was presented as world literature, so unfortunately it never occurred to me that there was anything else.

Still, the required survey courses were excellent; it's important to know, in a panoramic way, what's been done before you. I had always believed that, as a writer; it wasn't simply academic for me. I was curious. What had the poets before me done? We were *all* colleagues. I wanted to *know*.

It's integral to the education of a writer that he or she read widely in a systematic, chronological way—and in a way that lets you understand the relationship of the socio-economic-political context to what a writer wrote or didn't write. That is all-important. Writers and poets should also serve an apprenticeship, going through every known period of genre and imitating—and mastering—the craft, the techniques of that day, so that when you choose the way in which you're going to write, you're really making a choice, and it's not some hapless adventure.

At Chicago I read all of Thomas Mann, all of Aldous Huxley, and most of D. H. Lawrence. Those are three very different novelists. And because they and the cultures they wrote about *were* so different, the issue of cultural and historical differences became obvious to me. This reinforced my sense of myself as, so far, not publicly represented in the sense these writers were. I—my people, my gender—was not crazy, but simply not yet represented.

Two poets were very popular when I was an undergrad. One was Dylan Thomas, and the other was T. S. Eliot. I had memorized pages and pages of Eliot, so he had an enormous influence on my ear. But then I heard Dylan Thomas read, and I got very excited about him, because Thomas was going absolutely for the musical potential of the English language. Yet Eliot was also using language in a kind of musical way, an ingratiating way, a seductive way, to talk about politics and attitudes.

I began to feel very uncomfortable with my former placid adulation of Eliot's work. I wondered, Why is it that I know all of these lines of poetry from this guy? What does he stand for? I started rereading him for the *content* of his work. What was he saying? What were the implications of his work? Eliot, it seemed to me, was writing in rejection of the life we have, and that was hateful to me.

I became appalled by him; actually, I decided that Eliot was an appalling event in literature. And I decided that, between the two of them, Dylan Thomas was the poet who *should* be cherished.

To be a writer or a poet in this country is inherently political, but writing itself is not political by nature. Although I'm a political writer, sometimes, like Dylan Thomas, I just want to write about how light hits leaves or how the innocence of some of my students and the depth of their hopefulness will move me to tears.

I came to feel a horror about Eliot's seduction of me as a young poet, and this was very helpful. Consequently, I became even more acutely aware of the power of craft. Eliot had craft coming out of his ears—and to what purpose? To what purpose?

I concluded that I would have to acquire a comparable command of craft for *my* purposes.

It wasn't until a long time after college that I taught myself my own heritage as an African-American poet and came into an awareness of women's poetry. At Chicago I would go to poetry readings, and I would be the only black person in the room. And sometimes I would feel *so lost.* I would think, "I'm never going to show up to hear a 'great poet' and find someone who looks like me or who is talking about my life."

But then I thought, "Well, maybe I'm just going to have to try to *be* that poet."

My role now as a university teacher is definitely political. One of my most deeply held objectives is the empowerment of young people, so I see my work as a teacher as very much at the service of students. I'm constantly fighting for them.

The University of California at Berkeley, where I teach, is not a university set up for artists; like most of the "best" universities, it's dedicated to the dead. So it's incumbent on me to fight for the institutional validation of creativity on the part of students, as well as for myself.

Tave and I met one other time while I was still a Chicago student. I said to him, "I want you to know something. I'm going to be a very famous writer."

He said, in effect, "You're critically insane."

"Well, actually," I said, "I know how to write. Maybe you don't know how to read."

It was the first time I had had a confrontational experience with a teacher. Other than that, I had never argued with teachers.

But this guy, what he did, what he said, assaulted something basic, the source of my entire poise as a human being in the world. One thing I knew how to do was write, and he set out to destroy that completely, using his authority as a teacher.

Getting angry, though, can make you *do* something.

For instance, it's interesting that I'm the first African-American woman in American history to publish a collection of political essays (*Civil Wars*, Beacon, 1981). I'm the only black woman in the country who writes a regular political column (for *The Progressive*). I've been writing essays steadily; that's probably what's most distinctive about my public career, so far, as a writer and as a black woman.

And in Tave's class, we were studying essays.

When I joined his class, I was a poet. But in class I became aware that the essay form was mutable. And more than a century later, people were still reading the essayists, studying essays in a way that I had only, until then, seen poetry studied. I hadn't seen prose subjected to that kind of scrutiny. This suggested to me that prose might be a form not unworthy of my own efforts.

To this day, one of my two favorite essayists is William Hazlitt. He wrote "The Pleasures of Hating," which Tave assigned to us. I was a Christian and had gone to a Christian prep school, where hating was taboo; we just didn't do that. So it was a revelation to me to read this guy and discover his attitudes, his cherishing of hatred.

And it was obvious to me, even at nineteen, that the reason for Hazlitt's hatred was that his love had been rejected. I don't mean romantically. I mean the things that he passionately cared about had been trashed in some way. I thought that was very interesting. It would never have occurred to me otherwise, and certainly not at that point, that it was okay, even exciting, to be really furious, in a passionate, articulate way—that it might be useful.

So I don't think the course was a loss, no, and maybe some kind of ideology came out of it for me. I wouldn't dispute that. Maybe having somebody tell me that I didn't know how to write in my language, when I was feeling very vulnerable, wasn't a *bad* thing for me. It could have been god-awful, and decisive, but luckily, it wasn't.

I mean, it was shocking. At the time, I probably cried.

But I did give thought to it. As I say, I went back and told Tave, "I'm going to be famous." I wanted him to put money on it, and he wouldn't. I said, "You watch!"

Nobody had made me fight until Tave came along.

The encounter with Tave moved me from the passive place of having a teacher say, "This is really wonderful, you're really gifted," to my saying, "I am a writer. And not only am I a writer, but I'm gonna outlast you and the guys you're teaching."

That's moving very far along, you know what I mean, for a black woman!

Janet Kauffman

Janet Kauffman received an M.A. (1968) and a Ph.D. (1972) from the University of Chicago.

She is a poet and a fiction writer whose books include the poetry collection *The Weather Book* (Texas Tech University Press, 1981), the short-story collections *Places in the World a Woman Could Walk* (Knopf, 1984) and *Obscene Gestures for Women* (Knopf, 1989), and the novels *Collaborators* (Knopf, 1986) and *The Body in Four Parts* (Graywolf, 1992). She was a farmer for many years and is a teacher at Eastern Michigan University.

Though direct and down-to-earth, Kauffman seems often to consider what is possible, not only what is actual. She is a realist on generous ground, observing and imagining what could and what does go on.

JANET KAUFFMAN *An extreme ordinariness*

I think of writing as political activism, of a kind. Not that I believe it's effective as political protest, but it's effective for me. What I oppose in the culture seems so thorough-going—rewriting and rethinking things seems to me to be very active. In writing, I'm able to rethink things absolutely.

A short story I wrote called "Patriotic," for instance, is about baling hay. The story may not seem to have political content. But the idea that human beings can live pleasurably in the natural world—that they can step outside and do something, and feel at ease as themselves—to me, that is an ultimate political goal, where human beings actually partici-pate in the natural world at large. I mean political in that enormously wide sense of how we live.

My father's family was Mennonite, and I lived on a tobacco farm as a kid. Until I entered the University of Chicago as a graduate student in English, I had very little experience with cities. I knew I wanted to go to a city. I'd lived in the country all my life, and I wanted a graduate school in a city.

Everything in the Mennonite community was debated in terms of moral value—especially whether you should ac-cept into your life anything from the culture at large, since the Mennonites were so apart from it. Whether you had a radio or not, or a TV, were subjects of conscious debate.

That's important to me, outside of any religious con-text: what do people decide to accept into their lives? I tend to reject a lot more than the Mennonites do, in terms of assumptions about human behavior and societies. To a certain extent, they accepted the course of events. The world went along in a certain way, and everything was working for the good. I'm not sure that's true; it bothers me a lot.

I like to think of things as almost paradisal, not that I have any illusions about that. In the United States, *everywhere* is a godforsaken place. But in fiction I like those moments when there is a complete kind of human peace. It is so rare, and it is always momentary.

We're in the process of destroying the planet. The Midwest is typical. You see so much that's such a mess.

Yet people think better in godforsaken places. That's my idea of heaven—a godforsaken place! When everything's fine, you don't pay attention, whereas when things really are a mess, you can at least see it.

I wasn't actually raised in the church, but still, this ruthless sort of Mennonite moral debate, plus the Mennonite pacifist assumption that human behavior doesn't have to be violent, were influences that lingered. Humans and their relationship to the natural world and to matters of power are something I think about constantly.

I would agree that I'm as interested in individuals as I am in communities. Most of my characters are very strong individualists. This may be connected with the fact that I have often lived in fairly isolated places. The communities in which I feel most myself are small and intimate. Or, on the other hand, a sense of community that I feel strongly is an enormous, global one. It's not so much assertive individual differences that interest me, but the ways that human beings, as individuals, fit into things.

I had heard about the University of Chicago from a professor at Juniata College, my undergraduate school, a little place in Pennsylvania. I didn't know anything about graduate schools; I hadn't known anybody who had gone to one. So it was random chance that got me to Chicago. When I visited it, I just decided to go. I didn't know anything about the English department.

In those days, at least where I lived, women weren't as encouraged as men were to go to college. It wasn't viewed as a necessity; it was a luxury. But there was not too much I could have done if I *hadn't* gone to college. I really didn't have any interest in going out and getting a job. I liked school. I had a ball in school. It didn't feel like an intellectual decision.

All the same, it was an important choice for me to go to a university with a completely intellectual focus. For me, the concerns of language that came about through the study of literature and writing ended up matching the concerns of the natural world. With only *one* of those experiences, I would not have become a writer. The combination is what I think of as marking my work: an intense attention to the natural world as habitat, and then knowing how language matches that or makes a human connection.

Language has come to have a kind of reality and a physical property to me. I don't think I would feel that if I hadn't studied somewhere very different from where I grew up. As far as my own life and writing go, the elements that were most important to me in rural life, and those most important to me at the University of Chicago, go together. I need them both very much.

I was a French major as an undergraduate, and I didn't read much. I was very late coming to reading literature, especially contemporary literature. So the main thing that happened in terms of my writing at Chicago, or my eventual writing, was the discovery of contemporary poetry. I grew increasingly interested in contemporary poetry and language, and through my years of graduate study got farther and farther away from any kind of scholarly interest.

Language in poetry seemed like something you could *do* things with. I had never before thought of it in that way. In studying Dickens, for example, language always seemed functional, and I wasn't interested in studying it in an academic way. Without even knowing it, I was interested in language as a material for creating things. I found contemporary poetry difficult to understand. And the more contemporary poetry I read, the harder it was to deal with, and the more interested I became. Poets were stretching language, using it in individual ways. Language wasn't just something to communicate clearly; it was plastic and variable and malleable.

My dissertation was probably the least scholarly dissertation ever written. It was about the poet Theodore Roethke. Since he was newly dead at the time, there wasn't much critical material on him, and my dissertation was a study of his poetic language. One thing I'm very grateful to the U of C for is the freedom we had in choosing dissertation topics. I felt I could do *anything*. I doubt that I would have thrived in graduate school had there been obstacles and restrictions and pressures.

The sort of teachers who affected me most were teachers who ran classes like dialogues with students. Jerome McGann's class was like that, and so were a number of others—a course on the Puritans, team-taught by Robert Streeter and a professor from the Divinity School. It really seems important for education to go that way. I know it's the only way I've ever learned anything. Teaching and learning are just a process of talking. In my stories, it's the same way: people just sort of sit around and talk.

I teach at Eastern Michigan University: introduction to literature courses, women's studies, writing. And I also farm a little, although less and less. I'm converting my farm into a wildlife preserve of sorts. A lot of the land around here is marginally tillable, anyway.

I waited until I was out of school to write. I had written a little poetry in college, and a very few poems now and then in graduate school, but nothing continuously or deliberately. Almost immediately after getting out of graduate school, I started writing poetry. I started writing fiction in 1980, eight years or so after I was out of graduate school.

I was a very methodical person, and it was typical of women in those days *not* to do what they wanted. I can remember distinctly, once I had had my kids. . . . I'd gone to school, I'd gotten married, I'd had kids, and then I thought, at one point, "Oh, now I can do what I want." It was literally true. This was before the women's movement, and I didn't conceive of myself as able to do what I pleased until I had done all the things I was expected to do.

Only when I could get past the academic perception of things, and think of language and writing as a physical activity, could I write. It took me a long time.

Language just doesn't seem controllable. You can do things with it, but you aren't in complete control of it. I find that very important. What I'm writing now attends to language as a material. Anything in the natural world seems to have a complexity, an ability to be viewed in different ways. Nothing is certain. You can't just say, "Well, this is *this*." That pleases me immensely. It seems like an antidote to the way that so much human activity goes: in an extremely linear and clear-cut direction. Somehow, that seems very false to me.

In the course I took from James Miller on modern poetry, one of our projects was to look through letters in the Harriet Monroe Collection in the Rare Book Room. (I can't remember whose letters I was looking at.) I went in expecting to find letters where writers discussed poetics in intellectual detail. What I found instead was just ordinary letters, saying, "Look at this," and "What do you think?" And I *really* liked that! At first, I was upset, thinking, "I'm not going to find *anything* interesting to write about; nobody's talking about their writing." But the more I thought about it, the more pleased I was. I realized that writers didn't have to articulate *everything*. It really is important to me that there be an extreme ordinariness to literary activity, that it not be an academic matter.

Writing is often so pointless, useless; it doesn't *do* anything. And yet a sense of involvement and physical energy is associated with it. And I think that sort of involvement in the world is very important. It amounts to a redefinition of power. How can ordinary people, outside of positions of power, see their lives with some force? This is a study in vocabulary: What *are* the words that describe human involvement?

That's what interests me: to think of utterly redefined ideas of what it means to be powerful. And at times I have tried to find words not associated with the usual positions of power which would describe activity that had energy and emotion and power.

You have to live within the society you're in; to that extent, you collaborate. I live in a house, and I burn gas in my furnace, and I can't completely disappear. So collaboration, to me, is complicated: you live within the powers that are over you. But it seems to me important, in addition, to think of going the other way, linking yourself with alternative senses of power and, insofar as possible, seeing yourself not as a victim of culture, but as a biological part of things.

I have great trust in heading myself in directions that I need to go. I have always learned intuitively, bodily, that I know what I'm doing.

Janet Lewis

by Richard Stern

Janet Lewis was born in 1899 in Chicago, Illinois. She received her
A.A. in 1918 from Lewis Institute and her Ph.B. in 1920 from the
University of Chicago.

A poet, novelist, librettist, and editor, she has given lectures at
the University of Chicago, St. John's College, and Stanford Univer-
sity. Her honors include a University of Chicago Alumni Award for
Professional Achievement in 1982. Among her books are *The Wife of
Martin Guerre* (Colt, 1941; Swallow Press, 1970), *The Trial of Sören
Qvist* (Doubleday, 1947, Ohio University Press, 1989), and *Poems
Old and New, 1918–1978* (Ohio University Press, 1979).

JANET LEWIS *The poetry club*

The poet, novelist, and opera librettist Janet Lewis was one of a group of writers who came together at the University of Chicago after the end of World War I under the aegis of Professor Robert Morss Lovett. They called themselves the Poetry Club, and they published several small anthologies of their work. Others in the group were Lewis's future husband, Arthur Yvor Winters, who became a famous literary critic and professor as well as a poet; the novelist and memoirist Glenway Wescott; the foreign correspondent and memoirist (James) Vincent Sheean; the Pulitzer Prize–winning novelist Elizabeth Madox Roberts; and such poets as Jessica Nelson North, Gladys Campbell, Pearl Andelman Sherry, Maureen Smith, and Maurice Lesemann.

When it was decided to help celebrate the centennial of the University of Chicago with a book about some of the leading writers who'd gone to school here, the hope was to locate one or more people who'd been members of the club. None could be less than ninety years of age. I telephoned Professor Gelpi at Stanford and asked if Janet Lewis was alive. He said, "She's giving a poetry reading here next Monday." I wrote to her in Los Altos about the project. She agreed to be interviewed and sent me directions to her house from San Francisco on alternate routes, including a hand-drawn map.

After spending a night in a San Francisco motel, I took

This essay was published in slightly different form in Richard Stern's *One Person and Another: On Writers and Writing* (Dallas: Baskerville Publishers, 1993). Reprinted with permission.

to the road. Route 280, the Junipero Serra Highway, runs between the sea and San Francisco Bay, past San Mateo and Palo Alto. The soft foothills of the peninsula were brown and bare. Now and then fog filled some of the dips in the road, but toward noon the sun came out of the clouds, and there was a crystal brightness on cars, houses, and the large gray sculpture of Fra Junipero pointing west toward the Pacific.

The wildest surmise of the eighteenth-century Franciscan wouldn't have predicted the replacement of the apricot, persimmon, loquat, walnut, fig, and grape orchards by the electronic plants of Silicon Valley. I'd recently read about the serpents in this semiconductor paradise, the high rates of unemployment, homelessness, mental illness, drug abuse, and complexly fractured and extended families. Were these, too, the toxic waste of technological genius? Almost half a century before the silicon chip, Janet Lewis had written about ecological disaster, "the incoherent civilization emerging from the physical wilderness," in *Against a Darkening Sky* (Doubleday, 1943).

I took the El Monte turnoff, then drove along San Antonio Road to West Portola, near El Camino Real. A couple of hundred yards up the east side of the road were a mailbox, a garage, a grape gate and, behind that, the small, tree-shaded cottage to which Janet Lewis and Yvor Winters moved in 1934, seven years after they'd come to California. The door was opened by a tallish, straight-backed, white-haired woman wearing glasses on her large, strong nose; the face was serious, amiable, alert. The initial shock was, "This woman can't be ninety-one years old." In a minute you forgot age, though Janet Lewis moves and talks with that special economy of the long-lived. Perhaps because I'd read her work, I thought I saw an American Indian quality in its grace.

She led the way to a bright kitchen and offered juice, tea, or coffee. The upper half of the refrigerator was covered with color photographs of her daughter Joanna and her children, and her son Daniel, "who teaches French and Spanish and, more and more, English in a high school in Davis." One of the pictures is of a cat, perhaps the "morsel of suavity" about whom she wrote in "Lines to a Kitten":

Only the great
And you, can dedicate
The attention so to one small thing . . .
Kin of philosophers, and more, indeed . . .
You by your narrowed thought, maintain your place,
Pure quality of your great treacherous race.

Some of the photographs belong to Alva Henderson, the composer for whom she's written three librettos and with whom she shares the house. Alva came in briefly to shake hands, a pleasant-looking, blue-eyed man in—I'd guess— his early forties. On the wall was a poster of one of their operas, *The Last of the Mohicans.*

Janet and I took our mugs into the low-ceilinged, book-lined living room. I set up the small tape recorder (which proved more treacherous than any cat) and sat in what she told me was her husband's favorite chair, a wooden armchair with leather seat and back. He died in January, 1968, in his sixty-eighth year. In Janet's *Poems Old and New, 1918–1978* (Ohio University Press, 1979) the dedication reads, "For Yvor Winters Now as Then."

What was immediately clear was that though her past was rich, and richly remembered, Janet lives vividly, actively in the present. Though "I haven't written any poems for a year," there is one, "Trophy, 1914," in a recent *Threepenny Review.* It's about a cross found on the neck of a soldier dead at Verdun. "That war became vivid to me when we entered it. My brother went off to camp. Jim Gilbert, who'd been in the Poetry Club and who became a fine painter, also went off. I remember girls in the dorm wailing when they saw a friend's name on the casualty list. Later, in 1920, when I visited Chartres, the stained-glass windows were still in storage.

"I was supposed to go to Vassar like my cousins, but I went down to the university from Oak Park to hear my father read his dedication poem at the inauguration of President Judson, and decided, 'This is the place for me.' My father had come here from the East—he was born in Westerly, Rhode Island—with a Ph.D. in Latin from Syracuse. He got another Ph.D. at the University of Chicago, in English. I think he was in the first graduating class, in 1894. He taught there, and then went on to Lewis Institute, where he became dean. He loved poetry and knew reams of it by heart. I don't think he regarded himself as a poet. He wrote occasional poems, such as the dedication for the Ryerson Laboratory, and one night, at someone's request, he wrote the Alma Mater, which I read you're planning to replace. [We didn't.] He was close to President Harper and admired him greatly. I went to Lewis Institute for two years and took chemistry and geology—wonderful geology—but I have no aptitude for mathematics and never thought of becoming a scientist. There was never a doubt about my going to college—the university was always coeducational—unlike Pearl Sherry, whose father didn't believe that women should be educated."

"I've spoken to her," I said. (Janet had sent me her number.) She was one of two Poetry Club survivors in Chicago. The other, Gladys Campbell, lived in Hyde Park, and I'd met her years ago. She's ninety-nine, and had recently broken her leg. Said Janet, "She's almost immortal, but you better talk to her soon." I said, "I ran into her in a neighborhood restaurant. She was getting around with a cane and a companion. 'It's healing too slowly,' she said." (She died in July, 1992.)

Gladys had told me Professor George Sherburn had her read Henry James's *The Golden Bowl* in 1916. When I mentioned this to Saul Bellow, he said, 'My mother had probably changed my diapers a thousand times before she got through the first chapter of that.'" Janet laughed. "We read Henry James then. I don't remember Sherburn. I know Saul Bellow's name, but I haven't read him. We read Pound and Eliot as their poems came out." Her first book of poems, *The Indians in the Woods* (1922), contains the sort of imagist poem Pound was writing and championing. "I liked Eliot until *The Waste Land*. That was too messy for me." Yvor Winters had ridiculed Eliot's shuttle between classic appearance and romantic posturing: he enjoys "both the pleasures of indulgence and the dignity of disapproval." (Winters, *On Modern Poetry* [New York: Swallow, 1959], p. 71.)

Did Janet know Harriet Monroe? "Yes, she was a friend of the family, an energetic, feisty woman. I admired her a lot. My father took *Poetry* magazine from the beginning. I can't remember her coming down to the university, but we went to her house. We met Sandburg and others there.

"The Poetry Club was the center of our life. We did all sorts of things together, picnics in the woods along the river, dances in dorms and Ida Noyes. I invited Jimmy Sheean to a Foster Hall dance, and we also danced at Frank Lloyd Wright's Midway Gardens, at 60th and Cottage Grove." I told her that almost the first thing I'd read about the University of Chicago was the opening chapter of Sheean's autobiography, *Personal History*. "I never read it, but he was a wonderful man. I was closer to Glenway Wescott. After Arthur [Winters], he was our best critic. They're just issuing his memoirs, and I've promised to do something about them. There's next to nothing about the university in them, though Robert Phelps, the editor, says a bit about it."

I asked her about other members of the club. "There's Maureen Smith, a very fine poet who's been neglected. I wrote a little essay about her which the *Chicago Review* is supposed to publish. [It was published in the Winter 1991 issue.] And Elizabeth Madox Roberts, a great writer."

In *Old and New Poems* there are four lines "For Elizabeth Madox Roberts, Who Died March 13, 1941":

From the confusion of estranging years,
The imperfections of the changing heart,
This hour leaves only tears:
Tears, and my earliest love, Elizabeth, and changeless art.

How had the club started? "A student had come to Robert Morss Lovett complaining about the absence of modern poetry in the curriculum. Lovett said he didn't think it should be part of the curriculum, but they could hold meetings outside of class and he would act as a faculty adviser. I did have a writing class with him, and another with Edith Foster Flint. They were wonderful teachers. My major was French. Myra Reynolds was a wonderful teacher; I can't remember the name of my fine French teacher. Oh yes, Mademoiselle Pelley! When my father gave me a round-trip ticket to Europe and four hundred dollars for a graduation present in 1920, I was allowed to go because Mademoiselle Pelley was going, too. She didn't stay in Paris long, she went off to Vienna, and I got a job with the passport office on Rue Tilset, behind the Arc de Triomphe. I kept it till my mother came over in December. We toured, and then I went back to Chicago with her. I worked at *Redbook* and taught at Lewis. Then I got tuberculosis."

Her acceptance to the Poetry Club had been signed by its secretary, Arthur Yvor Winters, but they didn't meet there. He got tuberculosis his freshman year and went down to Santa Fe to be cured at the Sunmount Sanatorium. "He kept in touch with us through letters. He was our best and severest critic. He kept up with what was going on, the *Little Review, Hound and Horn.* I think he wrote for that. He read Rimbaud, Corbière, and Laforgue, though he didn't know the older French poets whom I'd read in class.

He was always on to anything new that counted. He discovered Allen Tate and Morley Callaghan and corresponded with them. When I got ill, I went to the sanatorium and we met there. I was on my back for two years and wasn't cured for seven. You have to be cheerful or die." Winters got his M.A. at the University of Colorado, and went off to teach French and Spanish at the University of Idaho in Moscow. They'd married in 1926, but Janet was too ill to go with him to Moscow. She did go to Stanford, where he went for his doctorate.

"We lived on the outskirts of Palo Alto. I felt marooned up there, and I wrote a story about some neighbors. The *Bookman* accepted it, and I felt I was a writer again."

I said she wasn't the only writer born in 1899 who grew up in Oak Park.

"Yes, Hemingway. I didn't really know him. He was around, but he dropped out for a year to do newspaper work, then graduated the year after I did. I was in class with his sister Marcelline for three years."

I thought of pursuing a comparison of their short stories about northern Michigan—hers low-key and a bit rambling next to his—but she took another tack. "I became a writer in the country, during summer vacations on Neebish and St. Joseph islands. I had a close friend, Molly Johnstone, who was part Indian. Her brother Howard was a wonderful storyteller. I wanted to preserve his stories about the family. I went at it in the wrong way, embroidering a sketch about Molly. It didn't make sense unless you went back and told the stories in back of the stories. These went back to the eighteenth century, to their Ojibway grandmother Neengay and her Irish husband John Johnston." Out of her research came *The Invasion: A Narrative of Events concerning the Johnston Family of St. Mary's* (Harcourt, Brace, 1932), her first prose book.

Of Janet Lewis's four other novels, three, like *The Invasion*, spring from actual events. "I have this affinity for the circumstantial case. I like to get at the intimate obliquely. Perhaps I'd have been more successful if I'd been more personal. Though my contemporary book, which is more personal, is rather shapeless." This is *Against a Darkening Sky,* the story of the violent accidents and unhappy love affairs which pound the orderly life of a housewife living in a Santa Clara County orchard. "Some of these accidents happened to our neighbors."

It's Janet Lewis's historical fiction that has been most highly praised, especially her second novel, *The Wife of Martin Guerre* (1941). Albert Guerard, Jr., the teacher under whom I read it in 1948, called it "one of the greatest short novels in American literature." Like the others, *The Trial of Sören Qvist* (1947) and *The Ghost of Monsieur Scarron* (1959), the book revolves around the misinterpretation of evidence. In a fine article on Lewis in *Dictionary of Literary Biography, Yearbook 1987,* Donald Stanford relates this theme to the arrest of David Lamson, sales manager of the Stanford University Press, who was accused, indicted, tried, and sentenced for the murder of his wife. The Winterses were active in his exoneration; Yvor Winters helped with the defense brief and coauthored a book on the case.

Lewis's reliance on circumstantiated cases as the basis of fiction may be related to her reliance on meter and rhyme, the need for an unwavering, authoritative control. In her later poetry, written after she'd stopped writing fiction, meter gives way to free verse, and the pure imagistic presentation is mixed with commentary and exclamation, as if, at last, a self drives through modesty.

As for her narrative bent, it was being satisfied by writing librettos. (Music is another form of authority.) Her first libretto, based on *The Wife of Martin Guerre,* to music by William Bergsma, was praised (by Richard Goldman in 1956) as "probably the most distinguished libretto in the annals of American opera." I did not ask Janet if these changes in her work related to her husband's death. In his lifetime, she too had championed poetry as the controlled expression of a rational judgment of experience, real or imagined. The poem was a public—so a publishable—celebration of the intimate. "It's an Augustan conception," I suggested. *"Out there,* public, formal."

"I'll go along with formalizing," she said.

The English poet and critic Donald Davie has written that her novels center about dutiful women who, from under the protection of authoritative figures—Martin Guerre Sr., Sören Qvist, Jean Larcher—enter into passionate relationships that threaten the authoritarian order (*Southern Review* 12 [January 1966]:40–60). Much of Lewis's invention in these historical "reconstructions" deals with passionate women. In the foreword to *The Wife of Martin Guerre*, she wrote, "The rules of evidence may vary from century to century and country to country, and the morality which compels many of the actions of men and women varies also, but the capacities of the human soul for suffering and for joy remain very much the same."

Now she said, "I had to imagine the feelings of these people in these situations. I also had to imagine what things looked like to them." Research didn't scuttle the imagination; it stimulated it. For *The Ghost of Monsieur Scarron*, she studied huge maps of seventeenth-century Paris. "When I got to Paris, I knew the Paris of 1690 better than the Paris of 1951. I guess I'd been thinking of seventeenth-century France ever since I'd done a paper on Madame de Maintenon at the university."

I praised the beauty of the Danish setting in *Sören Qvist*. "I've never been to Denmark, but I had a friend, an engineer at Stanford, who was from Jutland. He told me about the seasons, the way things looked. I've been accused of plagiarizing Blicke, one of my sources. Twain used the same source. Of course it's all in the way you use it."

The modesty of her excursions from the actual seems to me related to the modesty and sureness of her prose (and, perhaps, her being). It is clear, concise, precise, and quiet, lyric.

As Davie sees it, the novels exhibit "the dynamics of historical change from one form of society to another." So, in *The Wife of Martin Guerre*, Bertrande's love of the imposter who claims to be her returned husband is love for "a new psychological type," whose charm and decency may add the sweetness of deception to their erotic life but "disgrace the honorable family" and the social order on which it rests. My own guess is that Lewis's imagination took fire here and, in that way, she is on Bertrande's side, as—according to Blake—Milton was on Satan's. The passionate intrigues are the core of narrative power in all her novels, which doesn't mean that she doesn't dread the "incoherence" and "moral violence" which they engender. Her empathy only makes their danger more real. The tension between imaginative and, say, moral energy is what makes her a narrator rather than a social critic.

The third component may be her life as an educated, relatively independent woman who, for most of her life, has been a responsible housewife and mother. "Battle, murder, and sudden death, she thought, still did not prevent one from having to do the dishes." Against this dangerous sky, there is the relief of duty; and then there's the relief from relief.

Indeed Janet seemed relieved when the doorbell rang. The postman brought a large package. She stripped it open (brushing off my offer to do it) and removed an amaryllis bulb, examined it closely, and assessed its condition. The doorbell rang again, and again she got up with relief to introduce me to a lively-looking woman with frizzy hair, who left after a brief exchange. "She leads our local dance group. Three years younger than I and she can stand on one leg for twenty minutes."

Before lunch, which Alva was preparing in the kitchen, she brought me books of poems by Gladys Campbell, Pearl

Sherry, and Helen Trimpi, the poet who wrote the foreword to her *Old and New Poems* and with whom she was having dinner that night.

In the kitchen, we sat down with Alva to macaroni and cheese. Janet said, "Bless Stouffer's."

I exclaimed over the delicious cold persimmon from her fruit tree. She said, twinkling, "Most people can't bear the texture."

She and Alva talked about driving up to San Francisco a few months ago to see Monteverdi's *The Return of Ulysses*. They described the sets, the singing, the singers' gestures, and the music. I asked Alva how a composer, even one like himself, who had had two operas performed by the time he was thirty, made a living. He pointed to Janet, and there was a fine exchange about which one helped the other most. He said he'd taught a bit, but he couldn't compose when he taught. Now he was writing an opera based on *Tess of the D'Urbervilles*, doing the libretto himself.

Janet, too, had taught occasionally. "I taught Narrative 5 at Stanford."

"Why 5?"

"We skipped 1, 2, 3, and 4."

How about music?

"It always meant a great deal, but I don't play anything. My parents sang, hymns mostly. My grandfather was a Seventh Day Baptist minister. I'd have had two Sundays, but I didn't take to it."

"Are you a believer? I'd guess so from the poems."

"I don't go to church much, but I am sort of Christian. Christ without the Church."

"How about your husband?"

"I guess he was an agnostic. The most religious statement I ever heard him make was, 'I don't think the universe can be an accident.'"

On the drive back, the light on the hills was beautiful, and I thought of a line from one of her Indian poems, "The sunlight pours unbroken through the wind."

Morris Philipson

Morris Philipson received a B.A. (1949) and an M.A. (1952) from the University of Chicago. Since 1967 he has been director of the University of Chicago Press.

Philipson's novels include *Somebody Else's Life* (Harper & Row, 1987), *Secret Understandings* (Simon & Schuster, 1983), *A Man in Charge* (S & S, 1979), and *The Wallpaper Fox* (Scribner's, 1976). He has also written or edited numerous nonfiction books.

Taking tea with Philipson at his office, one gets the sense in him of punctilious organization—and the willingness to abandon it when a good idea insists. Philipson seems crisply, darkly rational and almost combatively polite. He is a challenging, witty, and sometimes merry interlocutor.

MORRIS PHILIPSON *Independence*
of mind

Nothing has become more obvious in the past two years, since the publication of Allan Bloom's *The Closing of the American Mind,* than that, for general purposes, nobody understands what higher education is anymore. Allan Bloom himself mistook it for the one true salvationist religion.

What kind of education does a writer need?

In *A Stroll with William James,* Jacques Barzun's tribute to his mentor, James complains that he felt deprived of a systematic education. He was taken from one country to another, was taught different languages and literatures, learned drawing as well as the sciences—all haphazardly. Barzun comes to the conclusion that this was the "perfect" education for a philosopher. There is a powerful lure in what's believed to be "systematic," but it turns out that nothing "perfect" can be prescribed or defined *in advance.*

How long is a piece of string? Answer: twice the length from one end to the middle. A tautology: the perfect education for a writer is the curriculum of experience and understanding of events that enables him or her to become the kind of writer that no other education would have made possible.

What attracted me to the University of Chicago was the character of Robert Maynard Hutchins, as representative of a center of learning that boasted offering the best education one could have. When I became a student at the University of Chicago I found that most of the student body were people who hoped to satisfy the ambition of becoming superlatively well educated. But though the ideal-goal was held in common, it was not pursued as a cooperative effort: individually the students were intensely competitive. The ultimate revelation was the discovery that there was as much competition, lack of harmony, and variation of beliefs among the *faculty* as among the students. Eventually you realized that there was no such thing as a unified conception of what that "best" education could be. In the end, you may have been left cherishing the same *ideal* as when you arrived, but you'd gone through an awful lot of roller coastering, intellectually, to discover what it wasn't rather than what it was.

To begin with, there were great exercisers of the mind—Plato and Aristotle. You went through various developments of thought as the activities of intellect were splintered into specialties. As for the roller coaster, there are great experiences of certain kinds of thought, or of trying to understand certain thinkers, that are exalting, that are euphoric. And then there are others that are very depressing; there are wet-blanket thinkers just as there are fireworks thinkers. All of these were going off all the time, not just in your own reading and thinking, in your own courses, but in all the operations of mind within everybody on campus.

At Chicago, there turned out to be no consensus, let alone unity of thought, and because there wasn't, there was no *indoctrination*. Where you have a school of thought, as in a school of theology, you should be taught to think in one way only; there should be a method of thinking, whatever the subject matter, that prohibits any alternative. That is certainly not what took place at Chicago. On the contrary, it was the ability to think on your feet, whether cultivated by professors in a somewhat nasty way—and there certainly were such nasty people, which has to do with temperament, not with method—or done in a very civilized way, that evoked the possibility of articulating your own discoveries and having them form part of an argument with others. Cultivation of a critical independence of mind could be thought of as the best thing that came out of this attempt to achieve the best education.

Independence of mind is a prime requisite for writing fiction. A novelist is independent. The way in which he does his work is uniquely his, despite the fact that it's done within a tradition. Within the tradition, there are various sorts of novels. These have to possess similarities; if a novel were absolutely unique, it would be incomprehensible. The novelist, remember, is not presenting the novel he's written to an authority for adjudication; the only "authorization" that matters is the effect it has upon a reader. And all judgments are ultimately personal. All intellectual achievement is essentially personal. Not truth or goodness or beauty, or any great abstraction of what might be thought of as the goals of academic study, exists apart from particular human beings. Without independence of mind, one would always remain a student rather than a judge of one's own work.

Everybody I knew at Chicago wrote. I wrote what I hoped would be a novel in my first year in the College, and I remember writing a short story that was published in the *Chicago Review*. George Steiner was one of the very first in our group to publish; within a few years of his graduating from the College, his first book came out. He must have been twenty-five years old. He was extraordinarily articulate, possessed of a great range of information, unusual insights. It was as though he was in touch with all the important ideas that were available to anybody's mind, even when he was twenty.

Steiner and Arthur Cohen—who later became a publisher, one of the founders of the Noonday Press—shared an attitude. Since they assumed that they would come to understand anything they turned their attention to, they behaved as though they already *had* studied and understood everything that was understandable. This was often a pain in the neck. And it was easy to catch them out, because they were always overextended. They were the kind of people who had so much intellectual collateral to put up for a loan that they could borrow on the future at all times.

Certain courses that I took and the way works of literature were interpreted have probably influenced either what I turned my attention to, to write about, or how I wrote. But I think this is entirely beyond my conscious awareness. I feel in conflict over the fact that education in general means the striving to arrive at an intellectual comprehension of some important subject (just as in writing fiction you must make sense of the complexity, depth, and range of human relations), yet despite that, it is a *mistake* to intellectualize the subject. Abstractions of intellect always make the mind veer away from an individual relationship and try instead to grasp general explanations. The fact is, it's easier to intellectualize something than to understand it in its fullest particularity. It is easier to generalize than to be true to the personal, the individual.

When you are creating something, you are satisfying needs of your own that you don't even know about. And if you try to judge that, minimizing an awareness of the needs that are being satisfied, you will only confuse yourself in the course of trying to bring about a work of fiction.

But you cannot avoid judging your own work. It happens as naturally as looking in the mirror and judging whether you look well or not. What happens is, you *do* judge your own work as you go along, and there are times when you judge that you "look well," and other times when you can't escape the fact that you are judging your work as "not very good." The main reason you might try to remind yourself that it is not always a good thing to judge your own work—or to *try* to judge your own work—is that it might stop you from going on and working more.

If you say to yourself, "I won't judge this until I'm finished with it," you are protecting yourself against the confusion that can occur between what you think something might be worth, in itself, *just* for yourself, and what something might be worth to somebody else. In that case you have to try to pretend that you *are* somebody else, and you risk falling out of touch with the sources that make the creation possible.

My deepest feelings make me an archaic character who would like to tell a story so that it will be useful in those situations where somebody says, "I'm worried about this or that, and I don't understand what to do about this or that." My response is, "Let me tell you a story."

As a reader, you first of all escape *into* that story. Secondly, you come back, knowing immediately why the story is relevant to you. The escape is very important, because *all* literature is "escape" literature. But you escape from yourself, from whatever you are at a particular moment, either into some literature that is beneath you, vulgar—which may be restful, because you're escaping from the demands that keep you highly civilized—or into a fantasy that might elevate you. Ideally, you escape into a realm of being that would be *only* better. You then walk back into your life, into yourself, as better for it.

For a novelist, the means of "walking back" is writing itself. The possibility of revising and reconsidering and recasting and "putting-it-another-way" carries you back. It means that as long as one is alive, there's always the chance to correct an impression, correct an interpretation—to be able to say to somebody else, "But that isn't what I meant! *This* is what I meant. Now do you understand?"

A continual effort to revise also renovates your mind and revives your life.

In having the freedom to try to draw the portrait of a character, a writer has a chance to examine possibilities, given places, given attractions in different directions, given demands that call for unfair or fair behavior. The novelist is trying to imagine what it would feel like to make such choices. Most novelists, if they're any good, can be depended on to make you feel what it's like to make such choices.

(Yet all the remarks you've ever heard along the lines of, "Oh well, the reason I like to write is that I can create my own world and my own atmosphere and get just the solutions I want, whereas in real life I never get any of those satisfactions" are, of course, also true.)

A further pleasure of writing is simply to be in awe that you yourself are doing it! And reveling in it. Or occasionally to reach that moment of self-satisfaction that Swift is said to have arrived at when he reread his early works, and made the judgment: "Ah! What genius I had then!"

However, ours may be the end of an epoch. There was a time before people wrote or read novels, and there may be a time coming when nobody will write or read novels.

It used to be that you could spend an evening watching a play and talking about that, rather than reading a book. But now you have plays going on twenty-four hours a day in your own television box. The competition for attention—easy as against hard—is so great that the novel almost always loses out.

How does a novelist fit into an academic structure? I feel invisible as a novelist at a university. At least they don't throw stones.

Although I'm aware of a few friends who have read some of my novels and talked with me about them, beyond that there are acquaintances here on campus who at one point or another say something as extensive as, "I liked your novel." And I ask, "Which one?" And *maybe,* just maybe, they'll remember the title. So I've learned *not* to ask, "Which one?"

Actual conversation—an interesting give-and-take about something written that they've read—has disappeared. I wish it hadn't.

The majority of members of the faculty have no use

for novelists. Even people in the humanities who might formerly have been thought of as interested in novels, aren't. They're interested in theories of novels. They read literary critics, and they talk literary criticism to each other, rather than reading novels. The novelist is excess baggage. And to everyone else in the social sciences and the physical sciences and the biological sciences and the professional schools—*they* don't read novels anyhow.

The investment in being "right" within a university discipline overwhelms the human life, the personal life, of almost every single high-powered, that is, competitive, academic.

I don't think there's any place for a novelist in a university community. If he has no success, and he has no otherwise-justified status in the faculty, then he is considered an embarrassment. If he is successful in any way, then he is considered a danger.

One of the earliest experiences of this sort was that of Sinclair Lewis. Before he became alcoholic and completely lost, when he was still doing serious writing, he was invited somewhere to be a writer-in-residence for a year—maybe at the University of Iowa. He found himself isolated. He was cold-shouldered. No one would talk with him—no one would *risk* becoming known by him—because they didn't want to end up caricatured as one of his characters in a novel. It's in that sense a novelist in an academic community is thought of as a danger.

What am I ranting about?

Ranting, obviously, is one of the pleasures of writing novels.

M. L. Rosenthal

M. L. Rosenthal earned B.A. and M.A. degrees at the University of Chicago in 1937 and 1938, respectively, and a doctorate at New York University in 1949.

His many books include six volumes of poetry: *Blue Boy on Skates* (Oxford University Press, 1964), *Beyond Power* (Oxford, 1969), *The View from the Peacock's Tail* (Oxford, 1972), *She: A Sequence of Poems* (BOA Editions, 1977), *Poems 1964–1980* (Oxford, 1981), and *As for Love: Poems and Translations* (Oxford, 1987). His most recent critical works include *Our Life in Poetry: Selected Essays and Reviews* (Persea Books, 1991) and *Running to Paradise: Yeats's Poetic Art* (Oxford, 1994).

He has taught at New York University, where he founded the Poetics Institute, since 1945.

In conversation at a New York City restaurant, he was alert, acute, and peppery, now jovial, now tart. He is a person of conviction. His pace is quick, his voice assured.

M. L. ROSENTHAL *A certain*
zealous intensity

We moved to Cleveland, Ohio, from Boston in my senior year of high school. It was my first experience of the Midwest; I hadn't yet heard of the University of Chicago. But I took the university's competitive scholarship examination on the advice of my new teachers, who thought the U of C the best thing that had ever come down the pike. And thus it befell that I came unto Chicago.

What did I find when I got to the university? I found the wonderful things that, with luck, you find after seventeen wherever you are. First of all, compatible friends, male and female (including the young woman I eventually married). And then, interesting courses: the surveys, and the discussion groups with their rather good young teachers, and the mostly fine introductory literature classes. And we felt privileged. It was still the first stage of the Hutchins era, and it was fun that freshman year to be selected to take part in the famous Hutchins-Adler seminar on "great books."

For me, the university was in general a tremendous experience, some of it marvelous, some depressing. Later adolescence has its peaks and valleys anyway—misery and ecstasy all over the place. Also, there was something formidable and alien in the quality of the university's intellectuality, and something fascinating as well. But that may have been because, as a developing young poet, I was always absorbed in everything subjective.

Not that I thought of it that way at the time. It's the sort of thing you see only in retrospect, recalling the oppres-

sive or heartening impact of this or that person or experience. For instance, I had nurtured myself on Romantic poetry but came up against quite different perspectives at
Chicago. Among the most important was, of course, the
so-called neo-Aristotelian approach—one that had its value
but was, at the same time, somewhat alien to the actual way
poems are made and the way poems live. So I quarreled
with myself and my teachers, and I learned a few lessons
from it all in the process.

The characteristic good teacher was very intense, and
insisted, passionately, that what he or she—almost always
it was a he—was interested in must needs be the world's
most facinating subject. And since he or she was clearly
right, I absorbed everything I could.

My own teachers? Certain of them were rather wonderful
people. No, Saul Bellow couldn't have been one of my
teachers. He was only slightly older, the friend of a friend
and floating somewhere outside my periphery. Walter Blair,
the expert on American humor and Mark Twain, was a most
kindly man: humorous, worldly without being cynical, and
encouraging. He had the character of a likeable newspaperman; and indeed he had once been one, I think with the
Chicago Daily News. Gerald Eades Bentley, the Elizabethan
and Jacobean scholar who directed my master's thesis, was
another such. Norman Maclean, with whom I played hand-
ball at times, was a lively young teacher in the humanities
survey. In the social sciences, there was the affable Maynard
Krueger, a leading figure in the Socialist Party. And I had
an outstanding biology teacher, Joseph Schwab. Also, we
all loved the grand old irascible scientist Anton J. Carlson
and, in the English department, the open-spirited Fred B.
Millett.

There were lots of good souls among the teachers.
When I was a freshman, I discovered I needed reading
glasses, and for the moment (a pretty extended moment) I

couldn't afford them. I was walking along 57th Street brooding about this, and Joe Schwab saw me, ran after me, and said, "What's the matter?" I told him, and he lent me the five bucks forthwith. A good soul.

Another instance. I had a most gracious graduate professor named Tom Peete Cross, an expert on Celtic and medieval literature who taught a demanding doctoral course in bibliography. In one assignment, he gave us a hundred or so problems requiring us to ferret out the necessary bibliographical sources. My typewriter broke down halfway through my report, and I completed it in longhand.

I handed it in to him with profuse apologies.

"Oh, I'm so glad!" he said, in his very Southern accent and breathing a faint aroma of Irish whiskey. "I'm so glad you did so much of this paper in longhand. I find typewritin' so hard to read, don't you?"

Essentially, the professors were all like that. What impressed me was their generous tolerance, which I'm sure I needed in full measure. They were a model I've tried to keep in mind as a teacher myself. Having a certain zealous intensity, I look upon them as an ideal by which to correct myself.

I was convinced of their very high level of intelligence and knowledge—but when my sense of literature seemed to be at odds with what some of them were saying, I went my own way. Mind you, they often tended to wear blinkers despite their keenly alert perceptions within their specialties. I was amazed, for instance, that people who spent their lives with literature had no real interest in the living poetry being created in their own time. You might call it the Academic Syzygy.

I studied with Ronald S. Crane, both as an undergraduate and as a graduate student. Now, Crane had a schematic approach to literature—he didn't know it was schematic; he thought it was inductive—in which he would ask questions of a literary work, and the questions were in terms of neo-

Aristotelian theory of plot structure. He was a subtle sort of Procrustes. I mean, the poor poem might want to go its own way, might conceivably not exist in order to answer his questions *in the right way.* Yet he was a brilliant man and taught us things we needed to know.

I once made up a little poem that went: "Poems are made by fools like me, / But not while studying for the Ph.D." It wasn't *quite* true. It was almost true. I found my studies most agreeable, an incomparable joy really, but never felt they were my whole aim.

Thus, Bentley once sat me down (I must have been seventeen or eighteen) to explain the mechanics of being a scholar. Very early on, he himself had begun filling shoeboxes with note cards of a certain size, doing one sort of thing with one kind of note card and another sort with another kind. He was a true scholar, for whom those note cards were simply a necessary device, and he was being a thoughtful mentor. Still, for my part, I felt they symbolized a kind of lifelong discipline I could respect but not quite make my own. And yet the benevolently formidable Bentley was in no sense pedantic or narrow-minded. Quite the opposite.

Thus I was introduced to the possibility of making serious choices, and that's a privilege—a privilege that often feels like suffering. Generally, you find choices are thrust on you before you're ready for them. This or that occurs, and you don't have any caution to fling to the winds anyway. So—here's something that looks as though it might be interesting to do, and you do it.

You ask about the Hutchins-Adler seminar and my impression of Hutchins. The seminar had a slightly philosophical bent, not terribly literary despite having to do with "great books." But the atmosphere was stimulating, rather exciting, because of an odd tension on H and A's parts and because our group was—or seemed—so highly selected. You hardly needed teachers!

Adler seemed rather supercilious, at least to my unfledged, freshman view. So, at a different pitch, did Hutchins. They sat side by side, talking in entirely different ways and sometimes at cross-purposes. Adler, of course, was a much more aggressive presence intellectually.

They were very polite to us. I think we'd been selected in two ways: scholarship students like me, and the bright children of rich or prestigious persons who might take a liking to the university and its interest through the encouragement of their kids. Or so we in the former category surmised.

Hutchins was a tall, handsome, sort of self-distancing man. He endeared himself to our freshman class by his ironic curtness in addressing us when we first arrived: "I understand you're the entering class this year. I'm sure you'll find that you will learn a great deal." And so, farewell—that is, he disappeared. He had a caustic manner that wasn't seriously caustic.

My memories of him are fairly superficial. Although I didn't see him often on campus, he was not an unfamiliar sight. He didn't go about engaging students in conversation and seemed to us to be leading a rather detached life. The students had some gossip going on about his quarrels with his wife, who, it was said, objected to his ever leaving the house. But this was probably undergraduate nonsense like the kind that fans circulate about glamorous movie stars. And they did seem glamorous; and besides, Maude Hutchins was an artist and thought to be a "bohemian."

Was *I* a bohemian? I think that, in the early thirties, it was a little bit like the twenties. If you were an artist of any kind, or dreamed of becoming one, it was assumed that you were a bohemian. And if you were a bohemian, perhaps especially during the Depression, it was assumed you were a radical. I guess I thought of myself that way: a kind of rakish angle to my bearing, but too poor to indulge myself except in being an adolescent and reading Keats. My sympathies were certainly with the left, and the Spanish Civil War had begun while I was an undergraduate. We felt, many of us, that World War II was inevitable if Franco's side, backed by Hitler and Mussolini, won out, and we didn't want that to happen. Some students enlisted in the Abraham Lincoln Brigade that fought in Spain on the side of the Republic. Others thought the brigade was too much under Communist control. Most of us were in fact fearfully ignorant about Spanish life and history, yet our premonitions were justified.

Ours was a very political age. Everything was charged with a political dimension in one way or another. Paul Goodman, whom I knew at the time, was one variety of left-wing socialist, but hardly only that. He was a very bright fellow who'd come to Chicago from Columbia as a protégé of Richard McKeon. He was so much older, or so we felt at the time, that he seemed half a member of the teaching faculty rather than a fellow student. I thought he was pretty impressive. He was interested in everybody's mind and at the same time tried to *direct* people's minds, and so he created an interesting little turbulence wherever he went. I didn't know anything at all about his bisexuality. (I don't know whether *he* knew about it then.)

The turbulence Paul created was, essentially, an atmosphere of intellectual pressure—pressure to grasp what other people were thinking and also pressure to argue things out in general and perhaps override the others. For example, he once edited a little magazine, possibly only one issue, and actually rewrote people's poems. He felt he was helping! But he was a brave and original thinker and made his contribution to the university's intellectual stew of Thomism and Aristotelianism and Marxism and logical positivism and whatever else that made the place so challenging. And the pressure I mention wasn't really just Paul's. It arose out of the Depression and the sense of coming war and the great labor struggles of the time, from the Republic Steel strike in Chicago to the rise of the Newspaper Guild to the triumphs of the CIO.

When did I start writing poetry? From childhood on I've always written poems, for better or for worse. But at Chicago I naturally still had much to grasp about poetry. That is, I needed to learn about letting go and, at the same time, exerting a certain control over the internal rhythmic elements of the poem and about helping it discover whatever it had set out to discover.

The most useful thing I began thinking about while at Chicago was the discipline of trying to close in on how artistic process works and on what a work of art—a subjective phenomenon but an objective manifestation—can teach us about itself. Art's permutations are unpredictably varied. In my criticism, I've often dealt with poetic structure as a living, changing thing, hoping to find out what I can from what I read and write.

Yes, the university experience must surely have influenced what I've done and thought afterwards. I used to stagger through the library overwhelmed with some poem or passage I'd just been reading. And so many of my friends seemed to be carried in the same direction. One of my close friends was Mark Ashin, whom I met in Blair's introductory poetry class, where we became enmeshed in a vehement argument about the relationship between poetry and science. (Blair was then a very new teacher and unsure of himself. He later used to say that we had scared him to death that first day.) Mark was a talented writer who eventually became a respected professor of drama at the university. The next year we were both admitted to Thornton Wilder's creative writing course, an emotional rollercoaster for me.

I should have mentioned Wilder, the only writing

teacher I ever had—and a wonderful one—earlier. He'd always manage to find some classic instance of the kind of thing you were writing. He'd read your story (almost always it was a story) aloud, or have you read it, and then would show the class how Chekhov had done it. He could do this in a way that might be humbling but was never humiliating. I observed no meanness in him, and he had no enemies save a few academicians who gossiped about him much as the students did about the Hutchinses. If he praised you, it was just marvelous. His influence was vigorous and even inspiring.

Wilder heightened my sense of the real thing in writing. This was a kind of qualitative leap, both because of what he said about certain subjects (such as the nature of sentimentality: "an overresponse to an inadequate stimulus" that "hits below the belt") and because of what those humbling comparisons of your work with Chekhov or Flaubert or his friend Gertrude Stein (whom he brought to visit our class and bully us with her Julius Caesar head and air of absolute authority) made you *see*. And so you knew that writing wasn't a matter of indulging your sense that you were a writer. It was something very different. In general, I think people's critical sense in that class began to outstrip their creative ability—especially in view of the university's whole atmosphere. They had to wait awhile to catch up with what they'd learned.

We, the student poets, did discuss our work with each other and finally formed a poetry group. Paul and Mark were in it, and Jean Garrigue, and, among others, Thomas Howells, Stephen Stepanchev, and Edouard Roditi. Jean's work already had its characteristic delicate sensitivity, tempered by an underlying realism. She was reserved, but she obviously ran deep and was as gifted as she was sweet-natured. Edouard Roditi, very elegant and slightly British-mannered, arrived with an entourage at our first group meeting and was introduced by one of them as a distinguished poet who *knew Auden*. But despite all that, he was a friendly and essentially unpretentious young man.

We were very aware of the city's literary identity and where the offices of *Poetry: A Magazine of Verse* were located. So near and yet so far—but most of us, sooner or later, were actually published in *Poetry*. Why should *Poetry* have gained the important position it reached? I think it was the new local realism, plus Chicago's urge to become a cultural center. The magazine's wealthy supporters and its ambitious intelligentsia sought something beyond the pursuit of money (in the spirit of some of Sinclair Lewis's writing). Usually it was women who started such outstanding publications. They had some money of their own, some resources, and heartfelt dedication. And Harriet Monroe added Pound and, partly through him, the whole modern avant-garde, to the magazine, side by side with Sandburg and the burgeoning genius of the new American poetry generally.

It would be impossible not to be influenced by all that and by so much more that one would need many pages to recover and describe. But in any case I began to feel afterwards, as writers usually do, that I was finding myself more and more. If I were writing about myself now as a poet, I would look at my poems and see what the development has been. No doubt studying oneself one poem at a time, in that way, would be a great objectifying process. But I don't know if I'll ever be tempted, finally, to try it. Better just to go on to the next poem.

Philip Roth

After receiving his M.A. from the University of Chicago in 1955, Philip Roth taught freshman composition at Chicago from 1956 to 1958.

His books include *Goodbye, Columbus* (Houghton Mifflin, 1959), *Portnoy's Complaint* (Random House, 1969), *My Life As a Man* (Holt, 1974), *Zuckerman Bound: A Trilogy and Epilogue* (Farrar, Straus & Giroux, 1985), *The Counterlife* (FSG, 1986), and *Patrimony* (Simon & Schuster, 1991).

Roth is an exceptionally authoritative person even before a word has been spoken. Intelligence is a physical power, as well as a verbal or moral one, and his intelligence—physical and not—is as salient and certain as a primary color.

PHILIP ROTH *Just a lively boy*

I seem always to need to be emancipated from whatever has liberated me. College liberated me from home. I had to be emancipated from college by going to graduate school at the University of Chicago. I was liberated by Chicago from home and college. I had to be emancipated from the University of Chicago by moving to Manhattan and going on to live for a while in Europe.

Now, when I look back on it all, I think, why didn't I go back to Chicago and be a writer there? Afterward I rather regretted that I hadn't stayed. I felt at home in Chicago. I've never felt at home in New York, and don't to this day.

The university and Hyde Park were good for me. Chicago, too. The high-powered intellectual center, the folksy, right-minded neighborhood, and the big city you could lose yourself in. I liked being the insider/outsider. All I ever feel like in New York is an outsider. I can't think of any other city in the world where I so quickly felt like an insider the way I did in Chicago.

I graduated from college in 1954, and went to graduate school because I thought I would be a professor and had to get a Ph.D.

I'd been to a cozy college in central Pennsylvania. I had some very good teachers there and all in all got a good education, but by and large anything resembling serious intellectual discord was buried alive, back during the fifties, under Bucknell's prevailing ethic of niceness. This enabled me to sharpen my satirical wit but I didn't enjoy much camaraderie or serious competition.

When I got to Chicago, I was thrilled by all the kindred souls. And there was a city—and I hadn't lived in a city since I was a kid in Newark. It was all exhilarating: the university, the new city, my new friends, manly independence. I felt that I was a man—and I began to write.

For the one year I was a student at Chicago, I took the standard master's degree program in literature. Good courses with Elder Olson, Morton Dauwen Zabel, and Napier Wilt, but also bibliography, historiography, Anglo-Saxon. Those classes were not for me.

I got to know the people who ran the *Chicago Review*. George Starbuck was poetry editor (and later was my first editor, at Houghton Mifflin). *Chicago Review* published one of my first terrible short stories—my first publication outside of the Bucknell College literary magazine. It's a story by someone who's twenty years old. That's all you can really say about it.

I got my master's degree in August of 1955. I was twenty-two. Then I went into the army. If I had not gone into the army, I might have proceeded right on for my Ph.D. It's strange for me to imagine what my life would have been like had I succeeded at doing that. But by the time I got out of the army, I'd become impatient with schools—or, rather, with schooling. I came to New York to look for a job. I was offered one at the *New Yorker* as a checker, and one at Farrar, Straus and Giroux—which later became my publisher—as a copy editor. But then I got a telegram from Napier Wilt, who was dean of humanities, saying there was an opening in the freshman composition program, and would I like to come back to Chicago to teach? I jumped at the opportunity of returning. I taught at Chicago for two years, from 1956 to 1958.

I was by then a little more willing to think of myself as a budding writer. In the army, I had written some stories, and one that had been published in *Epoch,* a magazine published at Cornell, was chosen for Martha Foley's *Best Amer-*

ican Short Stories of 1956. That was a boost. Also, I guess I was ripening. It was beginning to happen—whatever happens. I was more confident. And the university teaching job made me feel more adult. I wore a suit and tie. I had students. I went to committee meetings. I argued crazily about the syllabus. I even taught logic. *That* made me feel indomitable.

I had a little apartment across from Stagg Field. I worked until 11:30 every morning teaching three sections, back to back, of freshman composition. Then I'd hole up in the little apartment and write until I was written out, and then I'd mark papers with, I must say, the same ferocious energy I had for my writing. I was a very intense fellow. I saw my friends in the evenings. I was intense with them. Great fun, intensity, before it starts wearing you down.

I met Richard Stern that year I came back to Chicago, and Tom Rogers and Ted Solotaroff. All of them were writers or wanted to be. Tom was teaching freshman composition. Dick was teaching upper-level courses. Ted was a graduate student teaching freshman English in Gary, I think. They were all gifted and serious, and we became friends.

I was writing the stories then that wound up in *Goodbye, Columbus.* (I had already written one or two of the *Goodbye, Columbus* stories in the army.) One day, some six months into that first year, I had lunch with Dick. I told him a story about a family I knew in New Jersey who had plenty of dough and a terrific daughter. He was amused by the picture I painted. He said, "Why don't you write that?" I said, "But it's nothing. It's *stuff.* It's just where I come from." It hadn't dawned on me yet that it was *my* stuff. I remember Dick saying, "That's *something.* That's *it.*"

I went home, started to write, and almost overnight this stuff developed into the novella *Goodbye, Columbus.* Dick read an early draft. He was appreciative but a tough critic. We were working different sides of the street. Dick's approach seemed to me more literary than mine back then—I was tempted more by what was raw and vernacular. And yet *he* was the one who told me to *use* the vernacular material. I didn't trust it; I didn't *see* it. I suppose I thought I ought to be *more* literary.

Ted Solotaroff and I read each other's stories, too—rather edgily. We had a tense relationship but also a warm one. Ted, Dick, Tom, and I all gave each other pages and pages to read.

George Starbuck also read what I was writing. As I said, he later became my editor at Houghton Mifflin. When I was in Europe during the summer of 1958, I got a telegram from George saying that Houghton Mifflin had accepted my stories, which he'd solicited from me some months earlier. George selected the stories, giving the book a Jewish focus that the random group of stories I'd submitted didn't quite have. George, in a way, determined my future, because *I* didn't think that was my subject. I didn't know what my subject was.

I had nothing to do with any but literary or bookish people. I should say bookish men. With women I was more ecumenical.

Neurotic classmates? I suppose *I* would qualify. High-strung. Volatile. Opinionated. Argumentative. Playful. Animated. Quarrelsome. I'm sure I was as neurotic as any classmate I had.

I was instinctively fanatical about seriousness. Chicago didn't make me like that, but it sure didn't stand in my way. I wasn't a fanatical student—I was a fanatic about writing and books. I couldn't understand ordinary life. I didn't know what satisfactions it could possibly yield. Nor did I think that my fanaticism was extraordinary. I was in a community where it *wasn't* extraordinary. Hyde Park's the last place I lived where books seemed at the heart of *everything*.

I wouldn't describe myself at Chicago as "ascetic," and certainly not as a "bohemian." I was just a lively boy. (I think of myself as an ascetic *now*, unfortunately.)

One had to be careful about the temptation to become a gentleman. So many bright Jewish boys of my generation—and background—gravitated to literature because it was a prestigious form of assimilation that didn't *look* like assimilation. Not that I have any argument with what's called assimilation. I'm all for Jews reading Milton. But it was possible for even a Newark Jew to become a kind of caricature Noel Coward by virtue of "literary studies."

I wanted to be who I was from where I was. At the same time, I wanted mightily to escape those confines and breathe new air. Four or five of my friends—a small group of graduate students, of which Ted Solotaroff was one, and a terrifically entertaining and brilliant storyteller named Arthur Geffen was another—were able to make a lot of headway with the blunt neighborhood style that we'd brought with us. We took a lot of pleasure in having humble origins and high-minded pursuits. Either without the other was boring and looked to us like an affectation. Putting the two together was probably another affectation, but, if so, it was a *deep* affectation, and that's the most you can ask of raw youth.

I was an audience for their high-spirited exhibitionism and they were for mine. A lot of it was being boys together. We provided each other with an audience and with terrific fellow feeling. What feeling there was flowing back and forth! That's because we were still close to those street corners where we'd first exhibited ourselves. Chicago didn't put a damper on this kind of raucousness. It allowed for a nice amalgamation of the raucous and the serious. Superego Fights Id to Fifteen-Round Draw; Blood Drawn.

I met Saul Bellow in 1957, when Dick Stern gave a course in which he invited writers to come and talk to his undergraduates. I wasn't Dick's student; I was a colleague, teaching freshman composition. But when Bellow was coming, Dick asked me if, for the class, he could use my story, "The Conversion of the Jews," which I had written in the army and couldn't get published. It had been turned down by all the classy reviews.

I said, sure. I was delighted that Bellow would read it. Dick gave each student a copy, and I went to the class and sat in the back. (I don't remember whether, during the class, Saul knew I was the author or not.) Saul talked about the story. He laughed a lot and obviously had got a kick out of it. Then Dick and Saul and I had a cup of coffee. That's how I met Bellow.

I was so in awe of him, of course, that that meeting could hardly have developed into a friendship. He'd written *The Adventures of Augie March*, he'd written *Seize the Day*—how could such a person be your *friend?* Besides, he was eighteen years older than I, and when you're twenty-six and someone's eighteen years older . . . well, in the quaint old fifties, even a lively boy felt somewhat constrained in the company of his distinguished elders.

Was my life then simple? I guess it was. I wanted to be a writer.

It's simple before you're published, you know? It's simple—you write the things. That's the whole story then.

I prefer the writer I was in Chicago at twenty-three, even if I can't read his writing. But who doesn't? Who wouldn't? Unguarded! I was actually unguarded. Hard for me to believe. I didn't know who might be inspired by my writing to want to smash me one right in the face, and so I walked around with my kisser in the air as though I'd never heard of custard pies.

You know what it was? I was *stupid!* It was wonderful.

Susan Fromberg Schaeffer

Susan Fromberg Schaeffer earned a B.A. (1961) and a Ph.D. (1966), each with honors, from the University of Chicago.

Her collections of poetry include *Granite Lady* (Macmillan, 1974) and *The Bible of the Beasts of the Little Field* (Dutton, 1980). Her novels include *Falling* (Macmillan, 1973), *Anya* (Macmillan, 1974), *Time in Its Flight* (Doubleday, 1978), *The Madness of a Seduced Woman* (Dutton, 1983), *Buffalo Afternoon* (Knopf, 1989), and *First Nights* (Knopf, 1993).

Schaeffer's home in Brooklyn, New York, still holds some of the Victoriana she picked up from the Maxwell Street market during her Chicago years. The house seems full of curiosities, and Schaeffer herself seems full of curiosity. Appetite, large and idiosyncratic, has stocked the shelves.

SUSAN FROMBERG SCHAEFFER
Good behavior

The one person I didn't get along with at Chicago was Norman Maclean. At the time, I had no idea why. Everyone else liked him very much. We were a disastrous match.

What I must have wanted to do in his Victorian poetry class was write poetry, not study it. And I wasn't writing it; I wasn't writing anything. I had stopped all writing in my sophomore year, and I didn't think I was going to start again. To be in a class that was all about poetry was probably a very unhappy business. I was constantly reminded of what I *wasn't* doing.

So there was a collision of personalities. But he was, I think, a very patient man. He would have had to be; my behavior was reprehensible. I would always arrive in the middle of the class, after the quiz.

I wonder if this wasn't a case of two writers—two people who wanted to write, and who weren't writing—grating on one another's nerves.

Actually, he wasn't doing the grating. I was.

Later, when Maclean published his book, *A River Runs Through It*, I read it intending to dislike it—but I loved it. Of course, with my usual lack of sense, I mentioned certain lines of dialogue that I thought awkward and better off rewritten. I proceeded to rewrite the lines and mail them off. The correspondence continued in a quite friendly way.

That story epitomizes what happened to me at the university. I always felt that I could say what I wanted to say. It was never held against me. If you could, in the end, manage to do good work, that was what people cared about. There was no one way of being a proper student.

Teachers at the University of Chicago had tremendous reserves of patience, given the provocativeness of most of the students, and the bullheadedness of many (myself included). They would *wait*. And that was a great gift to receive, to be allowed to find your own way, not to be yanked by the ear and told that you must immediately do what someone else knew was wisest for you. Because even if they were right—especially if they were right—you couldn't have seen it, so you would have been forced into rebellion. That breeds a kind of bitterness, and in a very short time the rebellion becomes automatic.

It didn't matter what you wore or what you looked like or whether your family was wealthy. What seemed to matter was whether or not you could meet the intellectual standards set by the people around you.

I could also set my own standards. Really, you had to. Given the combative nature of students at the University, once you had set your own standards, of course you had to defend them.

My life began at the university; I was seventeen. It began with my discovery of freedom and tolerance. That had a permanent effect, one that eventually enabled me to express myself in writing.

Of course, everyone is born with a great many innate traits and abilities. And my family was so Byzantine; certainly I attribute to it my interest in what human beings are up to. My family and the families portrayed in Philip Roth's books are quite similar. In some Jewish families, there's always catastrophe in the air. It may be invisible for the moment, but it is waiting to strike. It can be precipitated by the figs omitted from a fruitcake, or by the death of someone in the family, but both events are equally cataclysmic. There is absolutely no sense of proportion.

My grandfather was pathologically jealous of my

grandmother. He used to follow her around. I was my grandmother's companion as a small child, so I was the recipient of all their stories—most of them quite insane, I later realized. But at the time, I thought everyone in the world was following everybody else around, suspecting them of strange doings. An innocent grandmother could have all kinds of peculiar dramas swirling about her.

Even when I was very young, I was highly analytic in my approach to people. I would consider others as if they were texts, which must have made me a nerve-racking child to have around. I would want to know why someone had done such-and-such a thing, and of course the adults would never answer me. Then I would be obliged to ask many more oblique and apparently unrelated questions, so that I could collect and examine the answers and come to my own conclusions.

Something about the university encourages that kind of individualism. People are attracted to Chicago for that reason. I certainly was.

I spent my freshman year at Simmons College in Boston. It was a disaster. Simmons was a school for proper young ladies, and I did not fit that category. They gave you placement exams to see what level of courses you should be in, and I placed out of many courses and wound up primarily in second- and third-level courses, for which I was rewarded with hatred by the rest of the people in the house I lived in. I could not wait to get out of there. I started asking questions about other schools, and finally someone said, well, if you want a school that's as different from Simmons as you can possibly find, then you should try the University of Chicago. She said, of course, everyone there goes crazy or has a nervous breakdown. I thought, fine, that's the perfect place for me!

I was accepted at Barnard and Chicago. There was no question in my mind about where I wanted to go. Barnard was still part of New York, family was around, and in those days it seemed to me that people in New York were overly concerned with good behavior, or socially correct behavior, and I was tired of all of that. Probably New York was simply too familiar. I was a fourth-generation New Yorker, and everywhere I went, someone from my family had already gone before me.

Chicago, for a New Yorker—even the sound of the word was exotic. It seemed remarkable that it existed outside of gangster films, that it could be reached by bus or train or plane.

I remember that first year in Hyde Park as a period of feeling fantastically and incurably stupid. Everybody seemed much more intelligent than I was, and I didn't see how I was going to survive in that atmosphere, much less succeed in school.

By the next year, I had very close friends. When you began to talk to other people, of course you learned that they were having fits of hysteria or attacks of fear similar to your own.

I remember reading Philip Roth's novel *Letting Go* during college, and thinking, that's my life. In *Letting Go*, the characters are struggling so in their personal lives. We all were, too. We were in extreme emotional situations almost the entire time we were at Chicago—usually embroiled in romantic entanglements of one sort or another. Not surprisingly, this caused a high degree of instability in daily life.

In some ways, I suppose, that made the academic experience, which at times seemed quite peripheral, all the more attractive, because it was rational.

I remember having to write a paper for Edward Wasiolek on *Moby Dick* in the middle of a major crisis: I was breaking up with a man I had been engaged to. (We afterwards got back together again, and probably that was too bad—it meant another four years wasted.) But the paper had to be written, so I locked myself in my room and said

I wasn't coming out until I had written it—and then discovered that I *had* no paper to write it on. In desperation, I wrote the paper on *Moby Dick* on the back of another paper.

Things always seemed to get done in defiance of personal upheaval.

I based the character Armand in my novel, *Falling*, on a friend of mine at Chicago. He was a Holocaust survivor. He would become involved—or try to become involved—with various women. He tried to become involved with me, then he did become semi-involved with a friend of mine. He would call at two or three in the morning, saying he had had a bad dream, or he couldn't work on his paper, or did I think that such-and-such a faculty member, who was teaching Coleridge, was on opium himself? Or he'd say he hadn't eaten for three days; he weighed about seventy pounds and was 6'4".

All I could think of to say—especially at three in the morning—was, "Go back to sleep! Call me tomorrow morning and tell me what you've eaten!" Because, of course, I wanted to go back to sleep. With luck, he would hang up.

This was often terrifying, but still, a lot of fun, although at the same time living from day to day, getting everything done, managing one's sense of responsibility to oneself, friends, school, teaching, was obviously a struggle. But the crises always struck me as funny, no matter how awful they were. In the classroom, it was just the same: our Anglo-Saxon readings, for example, always struck me as sort of a medieval *Brenda Starr*. The class was an exercise in lunacy.

Life was pleasant. I never had a sense of danger. We were all senseless, and I was particularly. My first year or two at the university, I finished working fairly late at night, and I would put on my trench coat over my nightgown and walk out to the lake, to think. (It seems to me I think better when my feet are moving.) Then I'd come back to the dormitory and sign myself in.

I had another friend who was thrown out of her apartment into the hallway, *naked,* by her husband. She called me from God knows where. Two of us went over with a coat, and brought her back to my apartment.

My closest friend was romantically involved with someone from the time she was a freshman. She wasn't Jewish, the man she was engaged to *was* Jewish, and his mother kept trying to break it up. There were incessant crises in her life, all very similar to the ones in mine. You could tell when a crisis in hers was in progress, because she would begin rearranging her room. You would open the door and find yourself in a sea of cinder blocks, boards, and books.

Everyone I knew was in a situation like this. We were also enmeshed in financial problems, but by comparison they seemed manageable. We were all one another's banks. Someone always owed someone else money or had just lent someone something.

The breakup of romances would often lead to people being incarcerated on the W-3 ward, a psychiatric ward at the university hospital. Most didn't seem to mind it. One person I knew seemed to find it a haven. I think what she objected to was that W-3 didn't remove her *enough* from the situation that had caused the trouble. (A bad marriage and an unfaithful huband.)

The university lured intellectual people who tended to be high-strung, sensitive, very bright, and often artistic, and who came to the school expecting to find kindred spirits and to find themselves under a great deal of pressure. Such people were bound to be troubled, especially at that age. I don't think the university induced the problems any of us had; the university may have prevented many others. I don't know what would have become of most of us if we hadn't had one another.

I don't know when it was that I finally felt at ease in the university, if I ever did. It was helpful, in some ways, *not* to feel at ease.

I started out as a premed major in the College. In the premed program, when you took a math course, you took it with math majors; if you took a botany course, you took it with botany majors. I always took an extra English course. I must have had suspicions that I wasn't going to finish up in premed. The training we received in the English department was fairly grueling—considerably more so than in premed, because there was so much emphasis on working independently. After that, nothing seemed difficult.

In the English department I encountered the University of Chicago's philosophy that you should not use secondary sources immediately, but instead should try to work things out on your own, and that it was important for you to be able to state a problem and solve the problem. Behind that, of course, was the philosophy that you could, in fact, state problems and solve problems without help, and that original thinking was important.

There was a high degree of specialization in many of the courses. I took some graduate courses in Shakespeare with Ernest Sirluck when I was an undergraduate. He was a Renaissance scholar and a wonderful teacher with a penchant for throwing erasers at his students when they yawned. Each time I took a course, it was in a discipline about which I knew nothing but which I was expected to master by the end of the quarter. You were expected to learn to use the necessary tools, to do the research that allowed you to become competent. And, to my surprise, it would generally turn out that this impossible thing was possible. I could do it.

After a while, I began to get a real sense of confidence—a confidence that there was probably no field, unless it was something like theoretical mathematics—that was beyond my understanding, and that if I became interested in a subject—even if I didn't know anything about it, initially—I could become, if I wanted to, expert, or expert enough, in the field.

When I began writing fiction and poetry, this was crucial in influencing the way that I proceeded. *Falling,* the first book I wrote, is the most autobiographical of my novels. Very shortly after writing it I realized that autobiographical writing did not really interest me. I was most interested in other people's lives, about which I knew nothing. Curiosity was to be the main passion of my life.

And so, when it came to writing my second novel, *Anya*—it is about World War II and what happens to one survivor of the Holocaust—instead of telling myself that this subject was impossible and that I wasn't qualified to embark on it, I felt strongly that I had taken on something very difficult but that it would not be impossible. This is another way of saying that the University of Chicago trained you to become stupid without being ashamed of your stupidity. You were innocent, you were stupid, but this innocence and stupidity constituted a challenge and an opportunity. It's terribly important to know one is stupid and to tolerate that knowledge. No one feels happy to find himself utterly uninformed, but sometimes it's necessary.

The same thing happened when I wrote *Time in Its Flight,* my third novel. I became interested in eighteenth-century New England after seeing a photographic portrait of a dead child, a daguerreotype. When I first saw the photograph, I didn't realize the child was dead. Once I understood that someone had gone to such trouble to photograph a dead child, I also realized how different the nineteenth-century state of mind must have been from my own and how quickly ways of thinking about the most basic elements of life had changed, and so I became very interested in that period and what it meant to be mortal—how people felt about being mortal in those times. That was something I didn't know anything about; I would have to find out what people's daily life consisted of, how people thought, what the influence of religion was, and what the roles of men and women were. So I busied myself with primary sources—with journals and letters and years' worth of newspapers—and then, when I felt I knew the material well enough, I began writing.

It was not simply the impulse to know and then write about these subjects, but the sense that they *could* be written about, that had everything to do with the training I received at the university. There it was assumed that you came in knowing nothing and that you would leave having learned a great deal. If it had been a different kind of school, with an emphasis on research and summarizing research and writing papers that were summaries of research, then I might have taken longer to become a writer.

And the importance of finding people with whom I felt at home for the first time in my life was inestimable. This happened not only with other students but with many faculty members.

So many people were such good teachers. There was Ellen Bremner, now Ellen Bremner Williams, an instructor. She was a revelation. A woman, doing such remarkable work! Every male in the class was in love with her—very annoying, since at the time I was madly in love with one of those men. I remember Ernest Sirluck telling me hers was the finest 75-book exam he had ever seen. My reaction, of course, was predictable. I thought I should never take the exam, because I would never pass it.

I thought Sirluck was wonderful. How terrifying he was! If you gave the wrong answer, he would throw things. Who could doubt that he took his subject seriously?

Arthur Friedman was very, very good; I took every class he taught and came close to writing a Ph.D. dissertation on Samuel Richardson. Wayne Booth and Jim Miller were my advisers for my dissertation on Vladimir Nabokov. I think everyone knows how good they are. R. S. Crane was still teaching. He was eighty-three; he was magnificent, a real master. I don't think I could have had a better training from anyone in logical thinking. Nevertheless, I was in a psychotic fit by the end of the term. We spent almost the entire quarter analyzing Browning's "My Last Duchess." At the time I didn't understand what he was doing—but Crane didn't care. *He* knew.

A professor who had a profound effect on me as an undergraduate was Edward Wasiolek. He was then in the department of Slavic languages and literature. I took almost every course that he taught: Conrad, James, and Faulkner; Tolstoy, Dostoyevsky.

Wasiolek was a fascinating, hypnotic teacher. When I came upon him I felt the way I imagine budding psychologists must have felt when they stumbled upon Sigmund Freud. The way he approached a novel was a revelation to me. It was the same way I tended to approach novels: trying to work out how the creature was put together, though of course when I began studying, I was still very much an amateur. I always think of the novel as a very, very intricate mobile. If the author does *one* thing here, then he has to balance that thing somewhere else. If it isn't properly balanced, then the whole thing is a mess.

Like a watchmaker, Wasiolek would take apart very long novels, *Anna Karenina, Crime and Punishment,* and then put them back together. I couldn't wait to go to those classes. The one time he missed a class, I did not hear the usual joyous noises preceding our escape into the quadrangle.

He also intervened directly in my life. When I first met him, I was in premed. I knew—and didn't want to know—that I wanted to go into English. I didn't think I was good enough at it. I didn't see the point of it, either. Really, I was hiding from what I wanted to do. I thought, well, I could learn to read books on my own, and in that case, why bother majoring in English? But Wasiolek suggested that I might consider becoming an English major. His method of working was, to me, the most perfect example of the Chicago method, and it was especially useful when I started to write. Once the writing was done, once the beast had come to exist, it became possible for me to look at it as if it were somebody else's text—to work on it with objectivity. That is enormously freeing. You are out of the cage of subjectivity. Moreover, you save a great deal of time. I have a sense of form, what I think of as a system of checks and balances, that is almost automatic. It leaves me free to experiment and to innovate and to change things around, to violate rules of point of view. When I begin to write, I often find that I'm *breaking* rules that I've learned. You have to do that. I know the rules about point of view, but they simply won't work all the time—they won't let me accomplish what I want to do.

When I write, I go through a process that I think of as emptying, becoming blank. If I have preconceptions, if I have "ideas" of my own, and especially if I'm not aware of what these are, then they can interfere a great deal with learning: they stand in the way of receptivity. I try to empty myself of all the things I know. There's no question that Chicago helped in this.

The critic in me doesn't come into play until a large section of something is written. When I start to rewrite, it's always like going back into a dream state; I dream the things that I'm writing down. This is not a particularly rational process. Often it's a two-part process: before writing, I think *this* is what it's going to be about, and *these* are the things that have to be accomplished. Once I begin to write, those things are present somewhere, but I'm not terribly conscious of them as I'm writing.

I had stopped writing as a sophomore in college. At that time, I was writing poetry, and the poetry was becoming increasingly cryptic. Somewhere near the middle of my sophomore year, it had become *so* cryptic that only I and one other person could understand it—and pretty soon neither of us could. At that point, I must have realized quite unconsciously that if I was serious about writing, I would have to find a way to support myself. But I'm not sure that alone would have stopped me from writing. I think that probably I didn't have anything to say, or I didn't want to say the things I could say.

I started writing again six days after the graduation ceremonies for the Ph.D. Once I had the degree, then I did have things to say. I felt ready.

I did start late. I started writing poetry again at almost twenty-six, and I didn't start writing fiction until I was thirty-two. So I've always felt that I'm ten years behind some of my contemporaries. But I really can't say I regret it. I don't think I would have done anything worthwhile when I was younger. I wasn't prepared for the self-exposure involved in writing. Probably that was why I stopped for so long.

I'm still very bad at even identifying myself as a writer. I prefer to be anonymous. I introduce myself as Susan Schaeffer, so people often don't make the connection between me and the person who writes books.

I have a basic dislike of the spotlight, of performing. In my case, writing is so private and interior that being out in public—where people are likely to ask you about what you're writing—feels like a case of radiation overdose. I don't take to it well. It's a shyness that one would hope would diminish with age, but doesn't seem to. What can be done about it? Nothing.

Even at Chicago, when I used to go to the library, I would photocopy all the articles I needed, and then go home and work alone, whereas everyone else would be in the library all the time. I would go into the library and see everyone there, and there they sat, covered with two or three inches of dust, and I realized that they'd been there a long time. And then I would become certain that *they* were going to pass and *I* was going to fail! I would be very happy to go home and do my own work without having to worry about what other people were or weren't doing.

I always found it difficult to work where other people

could see me. There is something very secretive about writing. Even now, I can write poetry when someone's around, because I write in a tiny handwriting nobody can read, and I'm relatively sure that even if someone could read my writing, he wouldn't be able to make very much of it. But if I'm writing prose, I have to be in a room with the door closed. If anyone comes in, I hide what I'm writing or I tilt the screen of the word processor down. No one can see it. I have hiding places for the manuscript.

Publication is never terribly pleasant for me. It ruins all these precautions I've been taking when I'm writing. I'm always happy when it's over. But I'm also happy when I see the book in bookstores and realize that it's actually "done." If the creature exists, that's always miraculous.

Some publication experiences are better than others. At first, it seemed simply a matter of writing the books, handing them in, and then everything would turn out all right. When my third book, *Time in Its Flight*, was published, I began to realize that things could go wrong. You could get bad reviews. People would not necessarily understand what you were doing. The whole situation became more ominous, more *real*.

But I'm not sure that I've ever been able to look at writing as "work," or as a job. I never thought of writing in terms of making money. Men tend to talk about writing in that way. I never have.

It's not a job; it's an inescapable impulse. Without it, I would be very unhappy. There isn't much I can do about that. I used to say that if someone founded a chapter of Writers' Anonymous, I would attend the first meeting, but now I realize I was wrong. Writing is too much like breathing. It would be folly to try giving it up. Of course, giving up *publishing*, that's another matter altogether. That, I think, would be possible.

People ask you questions like, "Who is your ideal reader?" Or, "Who do you imagine your audience to be?"

I don't imagine my audience to be anybody. I have a vision of things and try to put it down on the page. If someone else is interested, that seems incomparably wonderful and lucky.

I never thought of writing as a way of making a living. I always thought of making a living as a boring thing, something one had to do to keep oneself alive. This was my parents' attitude and the attitude of almost every adult around. My father was a clothing manufacturer; he had to go into "the place" every day. He had gotten a law degree, but he didn't practice law, because the Depression came along, so instead he manufactured men's clothing. I don't know whether he enjoyed it. He didn't appear to get a great deal of pleasure out of it most of the time, although he did very well. My mother, who was a Spanish teacher, was different; she really did love what she was doing. And many of her friends, who were also teaching, loved what they did.

Writing was such a specialized and personal and risky process that it always seemed to me necessary to have another way of making a living to support this . . . habit. It's probably inevitable that I ended up teaching, because that was the one thing I saw others doing that was really satisfying.

I decided to be a teacher partly because of the teachers I had at Chicago; their impact on me was enormous. There was no way I could avoid seeing college teaching as extremely valuable, if you could do it properly, if you were interested in conveying what you knew to students and in enabling them to learn to do what you knew how to do. The idea of teaching as power had never appealed to me, or teaching as intimidation, or teaching as the training of disciples.

My method is to let people exhaust themselves, to let them do what they're doing, and then if it doesn't work, they see it. Once they're exhausted entirely, they can be dragged up onto shore before they drown. If someone is bent on an obviously futile venture, you can *try* to point out that *this* won't work, and *that* won't work, but there is no convincing anybody until he sees it for himself. I think it is best to have patience.

Before I began writing again, I got the Ph.D., because I wanted the writing to be somehow inviolable. Of course, it never is, really, but you can give the writing a better try if you don't have to depend on it for your income.

I wasn't bothered by the idea of "critical" self-exposure at the university, not bothered by communicating my ideas about literature even if they went against the instructor's grain. I never thought of critical writing as personal. Probably I was naive. For me, the distinction between critical writing and imaginative writing involves what it is you must be faithful to. In critical writing, your primary obligation is to the text—to illuminate it insofar as you can. Your own personality is subsumed and the author's personality becomes paramount. The main task for me is to get as close to the author's state of mind, his intention, as possible, to get rid of my own notions of what he should have done, and to find out what he has actually done. This, of course, is an ideal. But in my creative writing, what I'm trying to be faithful to is my own vision.

These are two totally different moral imperatives; and they are *moral* imperatives. I believe that it's wrong to approach somebody else's writing and try to make it serve some agenda that I have. The writer had his own intentions, and if you have ideas of your own that you want to express, you should write something else and let the critic deal with *you*—in some ways a much more frightening prospect.

The moral imperative of writing fiction or poetry is to do the best I can. I suspect that sounds innocuous, but to me it's very important. If I say I'll try to do the best I can, I *mean* I will do *anything* I can as well as I can. Otherwise, why are you bothering people who are going to read you?

The moral imperative of writing fiction is staying true to what you have come to know. For me, this also involves an impulse to preserve things so they don't get lost. Important things that happen in the world are lost. Important things that happen in the world are lost when people die. That seems the enormous tragedy in life. It is one of the themes of my writing, but it's also one of the *motives* for my writing.

I want to know that I'm at work for intellectually respectable reasons, not creating fiction or poetry that is directed by cowardice or by some streak of good-girl behavior that's still there undermining everything, so that, when I write, I'm still trying to be *nice*. I never was very well behaved, but I think badly behaved people always have a yearning to be good—to get all the praise and approval that's always heaped on good little girls.

It's what I always think of as the Tina Pippitone Syndrome. When I was growing up in Brooklyn, there was a girl named Tina Pippitone who was forever held up as a wonderful example. Though it was clear to me that I was never going to become Tina Pippitone, for a time that seemed the world's most enviable destiny.

I left Chicago when I was twenty-seven. I still felt very much like a child.

Charles Simic

Charles Simic was born in Yugoslavia and came to the U.S. in 1954, when he was sixteen. He went to high school in Oak Park, Illinois, and attended the University of Chicago at night while working by day at the *Chicago Sun-Times.*

His poetry has been collected in *Selected Poems 1963–1983* (Braziller, 1985), *The Book of Gods and Devils* (Harcourt, 1990), and many other books. His translations include *Homage to the Lame Wolf: Selected Poems* by Vasko Popa (Field, 1979), *Roll Call of Mirrors* by Ivan Lalić (Wesleyan University Press, 1987), and *Selected Poems of Tomaz Salamun* (Ecco Press, 1987). Simic's essays have been published in *The Uncertain Certainty* (University of Michigan Press, 1985) and *Wonderful Words, Silent Truth* (Michigan, 1990). He won the Pulitzer Prize for poetry in 1990.

As a recent immigrant, Simic had an experience at the university which was less than typical. That was what he chose to emphasize, modestly but heartily. In Chicago at large, and also at the university, Simic was figuring out America—and himself. The stakes were high, and so was his energy.

My father was an optimist. He always felt like the money would just sort of appear one day, you know? "Here it is!"

But it never did.

He went along with everything I said, as long as I was healthy and did not break the law. In that respect, my parents were very nice. My father wanted me to be an artist of some sort. I studied painting first. He was happy about that.

When I was a senior in high school, my father, who at one time had been accepted at Columbia University—he never actually went—asked me to apply to Columbia, and I did. I also applied to Purdue and to the University of Chicago. I was accepted at all three places, but discovered that my father didn't have the money to put me through those schools. So I went to Chicago at night and worked during the day at the *Chicago Sun-Times*.

I must say, it was a very strange period in my life. I started college in 1957, an émigré from Yugoslavia living in Oak Park. I had been in the United States for only three years.

I never had much confidence. I didn't even raise the question. Everything happened so quickly. For a long time, I couldn't sort things out. I'm saying this only now; I wasn't thinking it in those days. It seems very strange that I should have come from this to that to that.

I just wanted to drift along. It was easy to live, to get a job. But I had no plans. I couldn't imagine what I would be.

We all came to America as if to an ideal. America was Hollywood, an incredible place. All American movies were made in southern California, and if you were in Europe, you were watching those palm trees in the wind, convertibles, Lauren Bacall, Rita Hayworth. There's something about the place that was very attractive, but also troubling. America was too much, too different, enormous compared to what I knew when I came.

There was something wonderfully reassuring, though, in discovering suffering humanity in America. You'd say, "Okay, *this* I understand. This I understand."

Chicago in those days was a scene that Dostoyevsky would have found congenial and familiar. Chicago was like Dostoyevsky's descriptions of the slums of St. Petersburg: there was ugliness, tremendous ugliness. And impoverished Eastern Europeans. Well, not so impoverished, because they did have jobs. A Ukrainian, let's say, would come to Chicago when he was a boy, get on a shift in some factory and then, because overtime was so well paid, stay for the next forty years. He would speak some English, a little bit of Hungarian, a little bit of Italian, and Polish, because he'd worked for years with those people. But these were the kind of people who were not at home in any culture anymore. They had forgotten their own culture, and they were not participating in American culture. Actually, they didn't speak *any* languages.

They became slaves. They liked the idea! They worked four extra hours every day, and they worked weekends. They just worked—all their lives. When you met them, you couldn't tell what age they were. They were forty, fifty, sixty; they had a gray look.

The Midwest was a tremendously prosperous place. Yet Chicago was odd, provincial in many respects. The Loop would be dark at eight o'clock in winter—nothing going on. If you went on the el, you would see women going off to the factories, wearing babushkas—journeys that would take an hour and fifteen minutes. You know how, in winter, an el door opens with a blast of really cold air?

And you shiver, then the door closes, and there's an artificial heat? It was money, it was work; people got along.

Whenever I go to Chicago, I feel at home, as if I could resume my life. It's not as if I would ever do it. But I know how the place works, who the people are.

Chicago gave me a sense of real America, better than if I'd happened to be in a small town in the Midwest, where everybody, the local pastor, neighbors, would have met me, would have been very friendly.

I wrote a six-part poem that describes a scene on Maxwell Street. I like the anarchy in Chicago, the sense of roughness only a few blocks from the lake—where there were gin mills, honky tonks, all the way down the Chicago River. Those were real dives!

In Chicago, you got a sense of all the streams that America could contain. As an education, it was vivid.

A lot of people were educating themselves. I knew many Chicagoans who were not from Chicago originally, or if they were, they came from the lower class. Eventually, they moved out of that; they wanted to educate themselves. There was a tremendous excitement about it. Everybody was sharing it. God, there is so much fun in the world of art and movies and theater and music. You wanted to know everything. I felt annoyed with myself anytime I would hear names dropped. Somebody would say, "Oh, I don't think Pissarro is as good as . . . um . . . Seurat," and I would think, "Oh my God—I've never heard of those guys!" So I'd go and look them up. You didn't want to be left out.

I'd take huge art books out from the library—just take them home and read them. I couldn't believe it. Take *ten* of them! And I did. I wanted to educate myself totally.

Once you get in the habit of discovery, it doesn't end.

As a University of Chicago student, I went to the campus on the South Side. After the first year, I went to a downtown campus in the Loop. I remember endless trips to the campus at night to get to my classes in Hyde Park.

By the time I got to school, I was tired, because I'd gotten up very early for my job at the *Sun-Times*. It was a union job that started at seven o'clock in the morning. Those were long days. But the good deal about the job was that once you had finished, you could leave. I would start fairly early and then kind of goof off for the rest of the day. I was responsible for preparing a section of the paper which consisted of classified and personal ads. It was a prestigious position—you met all these famous Chicago newspaper people. There was a guy called Irv Kupcinet. (Big nose.) Ann Landers worked there. These people were stars; you were almost afraid to approach them.

I expected that the University of Chicago would be a very intellectual place. I was interviewed by a young fellow—I don't know if he was an instructor or a graduate student or simply an admissions officer—and the first question he asked was what did I think of Henry James.

Henry James is one of the few writers I've never cared for much. Like root vegetables—I can take him or leave him. I found him just so slow, and I didn't care about the people he wrote about. In those days, I really hated him. So I remember having a very awkward conversation. I didn't blurt out, "Oh, no, I don't *like* Henry James!" But . . .

I took a course in contemporary poetry that stopped with Pound and Eliot. I remember wanting to write a paper on Hart Crane.

There were very large classes in the evenings. I remember the winter cold, and having to walk through the el and wait on the platform and go to the Loop. Then I had to change els to get to Oak Park.

That was an interesting crew of people in those big evening classes. I was more interested in the girls than in the boys. There was always somebody I'd accompany to the el, you know. . . . They were kind of touching, small-town girls whose parents didn't have the money or the inclination to send them to college. They came to the city and worked somewhere all day, as secretaries. Some were almost too poor for college. There was a heroic element in what they did.

I remember a slight jealousy, more than regret, when my buddies from Oak Park High School all took off to good schools. Before that, their parents had paid for trips to Europe. I was reminded of my poverty, of my immigrant status. I couldn't do what they did, though I found myself in their world.

I was divided. I was ambivalent, you know. I was embarrassed to be around ethnics. I liked to occasionally sneak in by myself to a place like the Drake Hotel. I liked nice places.

Oak Park was a very classy suburb. Mine was the high school where Hemingway had gone to school, as the teachers told us. I had had a French teacher, Miss Miller, and she would say almost daily, "Ernest Hemingway sat here, in my class. I taught him the French that he later spoke in France."

The most memorable part of my time at the university was a poetry workshop taught by John Logan. I wasn't a member of the workshop, but I sat in on it, because all of my friends were taking it. A number of poets gathered: Dennis Schmitz, Bill Knott, Marvin Bell, Naomi Lazard, William Hunt. A lot of people.

We showed each other what we were writing— constantly. I was writing bad poems, a lot of bad poems. I suspected they were bad when I was writing them. They were derivative. Derivative of all sorts of people. Every couple of months, I would be in love with someone else.

I had all these great friends: poets, would-be writers, painters. And I would see the guys and sit in on the workshop and go out afterwards, stay up late, and talk about poetry.

Working at the *Sun-Times,* I met an aspiring writer named Robert Burling. He was studying for a Ph.D. in philosophy at the university, and had a job as a receptionist for Marshall Field, publisher of the *Sun-Times*. We got to talking. He was writing poetry, and I was writing poetry. So we decided to split from home and live on the North Side. My parents were fighting, and I wanted to be closer to school and work and Chicago.

We got a little basement apartment that doesn't exist anymore on Dearborn between Goethe and Schiller. Though it had a gorgeous address, the house itself was a crummy old tenement, and our place was in the cellar. The Oak Street beach was close; we could go swimming. I met some more writers at a bar called Figaro on Oak Street. I met Nelson Algren then, not at that bar, but at some party a couple of times.

He was blunt and very nice. The second time I met him, I had *Life Studies*, a volume of Robert Lowell's poetry, with me; I had a friend who was a great fan of Lowell. So Algren said to me, "What do you want to read that for? A kid like you, just off the boat? Read Whitman, read Sandburg, read Vachel Lindsay."

I took him up on it. I was never very happy with Robert Lowell, anyway. His stuff was foreign to me.

Ours was a very small literary scene. We would have a party in a room with the lights lowered, maybe a couple of candles stuck in Chianti bottles, some kind of primitive record player, and records by Thelonius Monk and Charlie Parker. All the women were in black; it was the existentialist period. People would be reading Camus and Sartre. (Existentialism came to Chicago late.) And they'd have their hair in long bangs so you couldn't see their faces. They smoked a lot. Not much to drink, because everyone was broke. The drink would always be pretty odd: a bottle of rum or kirschwasser, something awful.

This was the hip crowd of the Near–North side, people who liked jazz. Among the older crowd were radicals, leftist intellectuals. There were interesting older people, too, at the university. In a course on sociology, old men who had obviously been in the labor movement in the past would ask tough questions of some young teacher: "Hey, wait a minute!" You know, the kinds of questions college students don't ask, ordinarily. Just because it's in the book doesn't mean it's right, you know?

In those days, much more so than today, intellectuals came from a working-class background—Jewish, Irish. They worked all day long at the railroad, the docks, being a boss in the union, or doing manual labor. And there was a tremendous wisdom behind them.

They were very pleasant. And they all had advice for you. They told you what you should do. There was a tremendous suspicion of the Eastern literary establishment.

When you're young, and even more so if you're an immigrant, you're looking for role models; you want to blend in. I was all ready to blend in, and these guys kept saying, "Don't read those books! Remember who you are! You come from the Balkans. You're scum of the earth!"

Sure. I agreed.

They were an influence on me. They prevented me from becoming a phony.

One of the temptations for an immigrant is to outdo the natives—to immediately get a three-piece suit and read Henry James. It seemed too genteel. I wanted something gutsy, fast, full of anger.

Even if I don't mention them in every poem, there is an America of hard-working people in the back of my mind. I do not forget them.

I remember once or twice being in WASPy circles of very informed young men and women who were graduate students, Ph.D. candidates. You'd sense that their dream was to be British. If they were ever to become writers, they would like to be reviewed in the London *Times* and be received at Oxford and Cambridge. They were sort of nice people, but . . .

It has always delighted me that I come from an "inferior" race. There we were in Chicago, sitting around, Polacks and Irish and Italians.

I never believe for a minute that I'm inferior or superior.

Those young men in the three-piece suits—they just didn't know!

Susan Sontag

Susan Sontag received a B.A. in 1951 from the College of the University of Chicago, and went on to do graduate work in philosophy at Harvard University and Oxford. The novelist, short story writer, essayist, and playwright has received many prizes and awards, including a five-year fellowship from the John D. and Catherine T. MacArthur Foundation, and is a member of the American Academy of Arts and Letters.

In her large, light-filled Manhattan apartment, books and papers were stacked up everywhere. Sontag's signature white streak in her mane of black hair seemed to hyphenate one part of her mind with another. Informality and warmth marked the conversation.

Her many books—which are translated into twenty-three languages—include the novels, *The Benefactor* (Farrar, Straus & Giroux, 1963), *Death Kit* (FSG, 1967), and *The Volcano Lover* (FSG, 1992); a collection of short stories, *I, etcetera* (FSG, 1978); as well as *Against Interpretation* (FSG, 1966), *On Photography* (FSG, 1977), for which she received the National Book Critics Circle award for criticism, and *Illness as Metaphor* (FSG, 1978).

SUSAN SONTAG *A gluttonous reader*

What led me to Chicago? It was reading an article in, I believe, *Collier's* magazine in 1946 or 1947. It was either by Robert Hutchins, explaining the aims and curriculum of the College, or it was an article about this eccentric place, which didn't have a football team, where all people did was study, and where they talked about Plato and Aristotle and Aquinas day and night. I thought, that's for me.

Not only did I determine I would go there, but I persuaded my three closest friends in high school to apply as well.

I chose Chicago because I understood the College to be different from any other college in the country (except for St. John's, a clone of the "Hutchins" College). What drew me was the idea of the fixed curriculum—*that* curriculum.

Going to Chicago was like finding home, the place where I would finally meet people who were interested in what I cared about.

I'd learned to read when I was about three, so that when I entered first grade able to read and write, I was immediately put into third grade. I had a very mobile childhood, and went to many elementary schools. Because I was skipped at another point, I graduated from high school just before I turned sixteen.

When I graduated, my mother and her second husband were living in southern California, and she was hoping I would not follow my dream. Her fantasy about the university had nothing to do with the curriculum. She'd become a California patriot, and Chicago was "back East"—very dirty and very cold. She insisted that I try Berkeley. Since I was graduating in January, I agreed to go to Berkeley for the spring term while applying to the University of Chicago for fall admission. Her hope was that I would like Berkeley so much that I would give up Chicago.

And I did like Berkeley a lot. I took some terrific courses in that first semester. I realized I could get a very good education at Berkeley. But I had been accepted into the College, as had my friends, who were graduating from high school in June. I thought, "It's going to be even better at Chicago."

And Chicago was exactly what I expected it to be.

At Chicago, in September, I took the placement exams given every entering student, which determined how many of the fourteen yearlong courses one was required to take. (Students took four courses a year. In the fourth, or senior year, one was allowed to take some electives from the graduate divisions.) Since I had already found my way to many of the books which were required reading in the College, I placed out of all but six courses, which meant that I had less than two years of work for a B.A. I was actually quite disappointed that I would be finished so soon.

I still have all of the syllabi—the mimeographed "Selected Readings"—for my courses in the College. They're compilations of the assigned literary and philosophical texts and historical documents. I've carried them with me through twenty moves.

I don't think I would have been any different if I hadn't gone to Chicago. Yet it was a pleasure to be in a place where there was nothing to ignore. This was a place where all one was *supposed* to do was study.

Until Chicago, I'd been a gluttonous reader. But the kind of intellectual work I was doing until I came to Chicago was simply *taking in;* I didn't have a method. The method practiced at Chicago was comparative, and basically ahistorical. Let's say you started with Plato—in the College, we invariably started with Plato—and you examined Plato's views on this or that, and then you went on to Aristotle, and then you compared Plato's and Aristotle's views, and then you added Aquinas, and then you compared Aquinas with Plato. There was a constant dialogue of texts; and the method of comparing them, which I learned at Chicago, is one I still practice in my essay writing.

A Chicago student was not taught to situate the idea or the spirit of a text in the time in which it emerged. You could be comparing John Stuart Mill with Aristotle, and you didn't think about the difference between fifth-century B.C. Greece and nineteenth-century England. So if there was any defect in the education, which I've spent, now, a lifetime correcting, it was the absence of attention to or respect for the historical context of ideas. It took me a long, long time to understand what could be learned by seeing how ideas emerged out of their historical and social context. At Chicago, texts were ideal models in an ahistorical space.

We were taught to be reasoners. We were encouraged to participate in class discussion, and one's contribution to discussion was judged by a very high standard. We were expected not to "answer" a question, but to present an argument. You would be asked to compare Aristotle's and Aquinas's ideas of virtue. You'd raise your hand and deliver a reasoned exposition that would go on for several minutes. The professor would listen and say, "How would you consider the following?" You were expected to be able to develop an argument orally and, when it was questioned, defend it with precision.

We were taught to be very close readers; we were taught incredible reading skills: to be able to examine a text thoughtfully word by word. (One might spend three class hours on two sentences.) It was the best education for learning how to read that one could imagine. But we were not taught to write. At Chicago, no attention was paid to writing skills. Of course, some of us became writers anyway, because the kind of people attracted to that sort of education are often lovers of language.

I had been writing—stories, poems, and plays—from the age of about seven. But during the time I was so sated and happy a student at Chicago, writing was postponed. One couldn't give oneself to this exhilarating education and then go back to the dormitory and write stories. Creative writing is a different way of thinking. (Writing comes from a kind of restlessness and dissatisfaction. And I was so satisfied at Chicago.) Besides, participating in the courses in the College was a full-time job—not to mention the classes in the Divisions I was not enrolled in but auditing, concerts on campus and screenings at Doc Films, and occasional forays to the Art Institute and the opera. I had no creative powers at all during that period. The university annihilated them.

I had been writing stories in high school, and I started writing again when I left Chicago. But the university was a total situation, a benevolent dictatorship. Which was fine with me.

The single greatest teacher in the College, and the most important teacher I ever had, was a man named Joseph Schwab. He was a teaching genius, the best embodiment of Chicago's version of the Socratic method. All I ever learned about him is that he came from a small town in Louisiana (he had a deep Southern accent) and had been trained as a zoologist (he'd done his Ph.D. thesis on fruit flies). And then he had come to the University of Chicago and begun teaching in the College. He was electrifying. Schwab taught several sections of Observation, Interpretation, Integration ("OII"). This was the master course, the philosophy course. In the second year, I audited the whole course with him again. I still think with tools I learned from Schwab.

Kenneth Burke was another great influence on me. I studied with him during my first year at Chicago, 1949–50, when he was a visiting professor and was teaching a section of Humanities III. That was one of the courses I was required to take (I had placed out of Humanities I and II, though I was auditing them), and it was sheer luck that I was assigned to the section he taught.

I remember the first day. The man standing in front of the class looked ancient to me; he was probably all of forty-five. I was sixteen. He wrote "Mr. Burke" on the blackboard. Then he began talking about the approach to literary texts he would be using. I thought, "This sounds familiar."

I'd already been reading Kenneth Burke on my own for several years—I read a lot of criticism and literary quarterlies. After class I went up to him and said, "Excuse me, Mr. Burke"—I was very shy, and didn't approach a teacher easily—"I hope you don't mind my asking, but could you please tell me your first name?"

"Why do you ask?" he said. I have to explain that at that time Kenneth Burke was not famous. I mean, he was famous to a tiny literary coterie, but he certainly didn't expect any undergraduate to know who he was.

I said, "Because I wondered if you might be Kenneth Burke."

He said, "How do you know who I am?"

And I said, "Well, I've read *Permanence and Change* and *The Philosophy of Literary Form* and *A Grammar of Motives,* and I've read . . ."

He said, "You *have?*"

Another miracle.

Burke was not a Chicago product—in fact, he'd never even gotten a B.A. But his approach confirmed the Chicago method of close reading. I remember we spent three months on one shortish novel of Conrad's, *Victory,* reading and discussing it line by line.

I had other wonderful teachers, too. There was Ned Rosenheim, who taught Humanities III, and Christian

Mackauer, a Hitler refugee, who taught History of Western Civilization.

Who else? At Chicago, I also audited courses from the beginning. I remember auditing English 203, a course given by the poet Elder Olson on the classic texts of literary criticism from Plato to Matthew Arnold, and several courses with R. S. Crane. And most impressive of all were the philosophy seminars given by Richard McKeon and Leo Strauss. I remember (indeed I still have my notes for) McKeon's seminar on Aristotle and Strauss's seminars on Machiavelli and on Nietzsche's *Beyond Good and Evil.*

I revered McKeon. But he also made me, and I think not only me, cringe. He might put a question to the class, a student would dare to say something, and if it were less than brilliant, McKeon often replied, "That is a very stupid answer." Or someone would be huddled in class in his or her coat—Chicago has very cold winters—and in the middle of a sentence McKeon would stop dead, and say, "Miss So-and-So [or Mr. So-and-So,] I'll wait until you take off your coat."

I was only auditing, so I never spoke in class.

This was a time when one never called teachers by their first names; of course, they didn't address you by your first name either. It's hard now to imagine this kind of formality in the classroom. The idea of being disrespectful to a teacher, or talking back, was unthinkable. Our professors were gods, and we couldn't imagine that we could have a social relation with them.

My attitude was that if a teacher was warm, like Ned Rosenheim, great. But if he wasn't, I could live with it—just as you shouldn't choose the doctor because the doctor is nice but because the doctor is competent. I was shocked and frightened by McKeon's manner, but I wouldn't have allowed it to stop me from going to his class and learning from him.

I didn't think, and do not now think, that the main job of an education is to teach the student to be independent. The point was to learn; you have your whole life to be independent. I thought *life* should teach you to be independent.

We still understand this with the hard sciences, or medicine. But with the humanities or social sciences, we think that all kinds of psychological elements should come into play, that studying should be a "growth" experience, that there should be "personal interaction," and that students should learn to be independent. Yet there's so much to be taught, and so much to learn, that if the teacher is teaching, and a student brings an attitude of respect to learning, then the issue of independence doesn't arise.

How can I say it? Since everything that was taught was praised, you learned all kinds of things were interesting that you hadn't *known* were interesting. You were always being stretched.

Of course, I disagreed with my teachers from time to time. But I thought the point was to get whatever I could from them. I *wanted* to be changed by them. I wasn't interested in showing that I was smarter, I was interested in learning as much as I could.

My main friends the first year I was at the university were my fellow high-school students who'd come with me from southern California. They were the people I spent most of my time with, plus some new friends I made at the university. One was Mike Nichols, who was a boarding-school friend of one of my friends from high school. My friends and I were effortlessly high-minded. We talked with one another incessantly, until all hours of the night, about our readings. We didn't have gym, we didn't have sports. (At one time, there were intramural football teams called the Platonists and the Artistotelians.) We were students, and we were studying.

Allan Bloom was a brilliant, real—enrolled—student in the seminars of Strauss and McKeon that I audited, and I remember him well. I deplore the vindictiveness in his popular book and the lament for lost (largely imaginary) privilege. I disagree with much of his use of Plato. I don't hate the young, and I'm not interested in promoting the fortunes of some establishment, educational or political, in this country. I don't have the agenda that he had. But like Bloom—and like George Steiner—I am a fervent defender of the mandatory curriculum, shaped by philosophical inquiry, and beginning with, yes, Plato and Aristotle and the Greek dramatists and Herodotus and Thucydides. I expect to continue to reread the books on this list for the rest of my life.

At the beginning of my second and last year in the College, I decided to sit in on Social Science II (which I'd placed out of) and had been auditing a section (I forget whose) for several months, when one of my friends who was enrolled in another section recommended hers. It was taught by an instructor named Philip Rieff, who, she said, was very good on Freud. And Social Science II had just reached the two assigned texts by Freud, *Civilization and Its Discontents* and *Moses and Monotheism*. So I dropped in on that section one day, and Philip Rieff and I married two weeks later. We were both eccentric, intense people. That changed my social life. And it eventually took me away from Chicago. The following year, after I received my B.A., my husband was offered an instructorship at Brandeis, and the year after that, after our son was born, I was admitted as a graduate student at Harvard.

Harvard was a superb university, but still, an ordinary university, with a big menu and no "right way."

At Chicago, we learned to read, to reason, and to debate. But we didn't write papers—we weren't expected to turn in papers any more than Socrates' students were expected to turn in papers. And our end-of-quarter exams were all multiple-choice, which means they were read by machines. The way I interpreted it was, "Well, these people don't care about tests. They're so high-minded that they don't take the grading situation seriously."

But I discovered in graduate school a whole dimension of teaching I had missed: doing a long paper and having your professor give you a close and careful reading with comments.

If my husband had continued to teach at Chicago, I would have been happy to continue there. I would have gone into the Committee on Social Thought and studied with Strauss and McKeon.

At Chicago I was handed an invaluable set of tools, and my enthusiasm and my natural respect for seriousness and for learning were confirmed. The University of Chicago was the single most important part of my education. My entire life has been a development of and a debate with the education that I received there. I think anybody who knows about Chicago and knows my work would make the connection.

George Starbuck

George Starbuck attended the University of Chicago from 1954 to 1957 as an M.A. student.

His collections of poetry include *Bone Thoughts* (Yale University Press, 1960), *Desperate Measures* (David Godine, 1978), and *The Argot Merchant Disaster: Poems, New and Selected* (Little, Brown, 1982). In 1993 he received the Aiken Taylor national poetry prize. He has also worked as a book editor, and he has directed the writing program at Boston University.

Starbuck is cordial and droll to talk with, a self-effacing satirist. The rhythms of his speech are like jazz. He is playful and critical at once.

GEORGE STARBUCK *Wonkiness*

Maybe I'm a real sucker for the University of Chicago. I feel the university saved me. It saved my mind from dullness and funk and mere self-concern.

What were my fears and gripes? They were commonplace, banal.

If I'd gone off to Chicago as a barely sixteen-year-old undergraduate, and a few years earlier, which would have been during the Hutchins era, it might have been too quick a force-feeding of the glorious Great Books education. It might have become an onus or a pall that I might have had to shuck off. But that didn't happen.

Those years under Kimpton were kind of nice. Everything was still proud and intellectually intense, but a lot of Hutchins stuff was being slowly dismantled or set aside. It was exciting without being monolithic; it didn't weigh on you.

The ideal thing to be at Chicago was an absolutely brilliant wonk. There were some people who stayed up all but two hours of every night, reading. *This* was the place to be bookish.

In the years before I went to Chicago, I thought I was going to be a mathematician. I was an undergraduate for a couple of years at Cal Tech, dropped out of school, hung out around Berkeley, and took a job as a rat breeder in charge of an animal colony in the state virus and disease lab. I fell in with some friends from high school who, in the intervening two years, had become underlings in a literary world.

I began taking a course now and then at Berkeley, and

a couple of times dropped out. I was desperately trying to invent what a bohemian life could be. And I fell in love and was unhappy in love—and, partly because of that, let myself get drafted. I had a reasonably happy time as a military policeman for two years in San Francisco, stationed at the Presidio, and then in Germany.

But the army was phenomenally boring. So I applied to a few colleges, and was accepted by Chicago.

I arrived in Chicago in the fall of 1954 with a heavy, heavy sore throat, got myself registered, rented a cold little apartment, and found out that there was so *much* to find out about—so rapidly. Since I'd had a little college before, I got myself admitted into the three-year M.A. program, bypassing the B.A.

I was living on the GI Bill. I didn't want to take part-time jobs if I could avoid it. I wanted to live economically. That meant I led the proper bohemian life. I didn't even bother to buy boards for bricks-and-board bookcases. However, to make ends meet, I wound up with jobs in the university laboratories. I was tormenting lots of small mice. I had credentials; I'd been an honest mouse-tormenter out in Berkeley.

I managed to get myself married, too, because my old girlfriend from California suddenly hopped on a bus and came out to Chicago. Within a few months, we were married. That meant I could qualify to get into one of those refurbished army barracks at the university, into the organized bohemia of a graduate-student village. Have a child, have another child.

I didn't feel like a serious writer; I didn't feel I was up to that yet. At Chicago, I wanted to get serious about literature, to catch up. I knew a lot of nothing about a lot of things. People had to tell me to read *Augie March*.

What I found was an English department that seemed to be riven between some fearsome "Aristotelian" theorists—Elder Olson and Richard McKeon—and some good old boys who merely did descriptive, historical thinking and writing, like the chairman, Walter Blair. And some other odd and interesting people who pursued specialties, like James H. Sledd, a descriptive linguist.

I determined that I was going to try the most fearsome of the Aristotelians, Elder Olson himself. He had a reputation as a martinet. It was known that he had published a couple of volumes of poems, and he had published a book on Dylan Thomas, who was still new enough to be exciting.

Within a few months, I began to learn how lucky I was that this batch of theorists focused on what literature *is*. They focused realistically on writers and their audience, writers within a social situation, within a culture. I took to all that while being a snotty youth and finding ways of differing loudly with my teachers.

Olson came on strong with very odd opinions. He thought A. E. Housman's "To An Athlete Dying Young" was one of the great poems of the nineteenth century. I thought it was silly. And yet, whenever Olson went into detail about language, the poetry would light up. He was amazingly quick and perceptive.

Ernest Sirluck stood out. He taught me a course in Shakespeare. He was aware that there were creative writing types around, and he tried hard to persuade me that it was better to be a scholar. He didn't persuade me. But I rapidly began to feel that whatever I might learn about writing I would learn best from exactly this kind of man. Obnoxious taskmasters like Sirluck did me a great deal of good. I still feel steeped in the seventeenth-century English poets.

Sirluck also singled me out and lured me into a public confab in front of the class about the fact that his swivel chair had a squeaky wheel. He got me to agree that I would see to it that it was oiled. There was a slight but awful Anthony Hopkins aura of decadent menace about this.

I wouldn't hold Chicago up as a Platonic model of what the academy for young writers ought to be. But what happened there was good, partly because it wasn't confined within a creative writing program. The best, most useful teaching that I got, and some of the most useful teaching that I see other people getting now, toward being a writer, is not working over would-be poem manuscripts. It is just teaching how to read, teaching what literature is, what its resonances and meanings and uses can be.

James Sledd was a man whose whole life had been spent in absorbing more and more of the English language—the varieties of it. He was wonderful. He was a Southerner, laconic-seeming, with a clear, high, reedy voice. I admired him, but I also came to realize that there was more than one way of being a genuine suitor of language, being genuinely gaga over that human artifact.

Then there were guys like Stuart Tave, who taught the most daunting kind of course, where you had to read one long Victorian novel per week. He was so businesslike and so kindly and yet so absolutely without grandeur.

Another lofty person was Morton Dauwen Zabel. Zabel was very proud of himself and proud of his firsthand knowledge of modern poetry and poets. He got my attention by turning to one of my favorite Gerard Manley Hopkins poems, a sonnet. He gave a long disquisition about the sprung rhythm of it and carefully adumbrated a description of what kind of a variation on a five-stress iambic this was. But the poem happens to be in hexameters; it happens to be in a *six*-stress line. I could show this old fart up! Cheap thrill treasured forever after.

Years later, I discovered that the young Morton Dauwen Zabel had been an editor of *Poetry* magazine, smart as a whip, an opportunist on behalf of the best and likeliest of the new modernisms as they arose. What I had yapped at in Wieboldt was a husk, a wisp, a wraith, sleepwalking the last three years toward a decent retirement.

There also was one really silly, dandified, overweening old dud in the department. And there was the guy I took eighteenth-century literature from, who, it became clear, had charmingly lost interest in eighteenth-century drama twenty years before. What he enjoyed reading, and read himself to sleep with every evening, was mediocre mystery novels. He had lectures he would read to us, and was utterly incapable of responding to things. These were the accidents of an open and syncretic and deliberately varied bill of fare.

At every step I was aware of things abroad elsewhere in town. Geniuses at the Blue Note. The ferocious Algren. My friend Dave Ray, another student, had had beers with the man. He *existed.* James T. Farrell lived, breathed, and still hacked new grit-novels out of the stone of his childhood.

There was, on the other hand, *Poetry* magazine, which was in the care of Henry Rago at that time. A nice guy, Rago was very sentimentally attached to the magazine, and was a rather sentimental poet himself—but just as earnest as could be about trying to foster young talent. I don't know how he stood it, but he always had a kind word and an open door and even a free sandwich for young would-be writers and editors who came by. One also saw what it took out of a man to be constantly cosseting patrons. In those days, Ellen Borden Stevenson was *Poetry*'s big, difficult patron. She was Mrs. Adlai Stevenson, and was one of the heirs and heiresses of Borden's milk. She would insist on being at the center of poetry reading evenings, and she was always promising more subvention—little paychecks, and things like that—which she would never get around to making good on. It was very definitely an old-fashioned kind of social lionizing that she wanted to do. Henry Rago had to praise her at every turn; we twerps didn't.

Don't be an editor, we told each other. Starve in Tangier, sell shoes, don't be a damn editor. Hell, even teach English. Editor, Prof. The fate of so many of us.

The downtown College was expanding, and its adult education humanities programs were being designed by a brilliant young teacher—a teacher with a capital "t." Teaching was his vocation. He was famous for his syllabi and for getting the overworked Ph.D.-candidate "assistants" on his staff to teach like angels and like it. They all liked working for this guy, no older than they were, who was also sort of a poet, one heard, and was published in magazines. His name was Galway Kinnell.

I remember hearing a couple of the older graduate students wondering whether Robert Maynard Hutchins at that age might have had the same kind of sexiness and bemusement as Kinnell. It has astonished me ever since that he jerked himself out of that rut, staying away from academic jobs for almost twenty years while he took his full flier on being a poet.

The university would bring writers in, just as they brought in great performing musicians, and set them up at the lit end of the fine, widened, wild Victorian-gothic cave of Mandel Hall. T. S. Eliot and e. e. cummings came— cummings *not* dead, absolutely tall and commanding, and disturbingly like a colonel in the U.S. army: hair cut very short, utterly erect bearing, and no schmoozing around or cracking extraneous wise remarks between the poems. Marianne Moore came, and so did William Carlos Williams.

Williams visited under the auspices of the English department. People were beginning to wake up to the fact that he was singular and wonderful and perhaps great, but he hadn't solidified a reputation yet alongside Eliot and Stevens and Company. They set him up in Rockefeller Chapel. *Hyper*cavernous, but they had a good mike for him. This was a few years before he died, and his palsy gave him a little trouble speaking; you could see leftover effects of a couple of strokes. But he was all there, and it was a moving performance.

If only I had taken a cagey side seat where I could have watched audience reaction, then I might have noticed Galway Kinnell, who was at the reading, either taking notes or not taking notes toward a poem he published soon after—a poem about William Carlos Williams reading in Rockefeller Chapel. The first or second sentence begins, "Your honesty built you a tower," and it winds up cocking a snook at the whole damn English department, the whole damn university, the whole damn occasion, with a sardonic description of a wretched "professor," unmistakably Elder Olson, though not named, who knocked spittle from his pipe, then scrammed.

One of my favorite American poets, William Harmon, went through Chicago about a decade after and got his Ph.D. His first book, *Treasury Holiday,* is a big, mock-Whitmanesque ode to the United States at the time of the Vietnam War, in which Harmon served as a naval officer. It alternates between bitterness and high jinks. In the course of it, he salts in a set of four or five University of Chicago poems. There's a lovely one evoking Norman Maclean. The nasty one is about Morton Dauwen Zabel. Like Kinnell-on-Olson. Archetypal Chicago quiz-kid cathartic gesture. Harmon may be the finest poet Chicago has produced. And he's a wise guy and a world-class scholar-philologist. Next to him, there's Bill Knott, untouched by the university, imbued with utterly inspired bookishness, wonkiness, but also a real indigene, a voice from Chicago, Illinois.

I was unpaid help for two years at the *Chicago Review.* And in the *Chicago Review* crowd, there was Chip Karmatz, who took the trouble to look like a young editor out of *The Front Page.* If he had had a fedora, it would have been crushed, and worn on the back of his head, and thrown, on occasion. He liked to sit in the *Chicago Review* offices with his shirt partly unbuttoned and his tie on but askew, handling two phone calls at once, East and West coasts, because nobody had told him he couldn't badger e. e. cummings for poems or Rexroth for a think piece.

The *Chicago Review* correspondence with cummings

taught me a lot, just by reminding me that weird, grumpy, fallible, interesting, show-offy human beings were the people who produced poems. Even somebody who's aged and sixty years old and already in all the anthologies was as touchy as could be.

One of Chip Karmatz's assistant editors was the poet David Ray. He was a premature environmentalist. He claimed inner somatic certainty that we were all getting killed by the exhaust from diesel buses. We kidded him, joshed him, really tried desperately to shut him *up*. People who didn't know him would think we were palling around with some *paranoid*. Sorry, David. You were mostly right about politics, and beauty, too.

Dave had also noticed, and made me notice, that Chicago just then was becoming a fine theater town. Being at the University of Chicago meant you were reading and thinking about Brecht and his methods, his predilections. You were thinking about Ibsen; you were thinking about Shaw. You were thinking about the whole load of unconscious social history and social issues that underlay the Broadway stage— and what succeeded on it and what didn't. (And why aesthetically and why classwise and why lootwise.)

The university's drama department was terrific, but so were the Compass Players. A student—it might have been Philip Roth—took me off to a party once, and there were Nichols and May. I remember the book-lined, smoky, slightly seedy graduate student flat, and the fact that Elaine May and Mike Nichols were not there doing shtick or busking or going around checking on their vibes as performers— far from it. They just seemed to be enjoying the usual kind of *Partisan Review*-crowd yakety-yak about politics and the novel and Freudianism and everything else.

David Ray and I were taking most of the same classes; we had entered at the same time, and had the same status as mediocre but promising graduate students. I mean mediocre in terms of academic preparation. I'm not trying to be false-modest. There were many more brilliant graduate students—Phil Roth, Mike Fixler.

One graduate student who didn't stay long was Ted Solotaroff. He departed without having his Ph.D., realizing he didn't want it. He went to New York City and a timely connection with Norman Podhoretz's *Commentary* magazine when it was fresh, and then got into a very successful editing career which he's just stepped aside from.

Bellow passed through. Bellow indeed taught a course, thanks to a brand-new, not-yet-dry-behind-the-ears assistant professor in the department, Dick Stern. Stern came in all big, bluff, articulate, and ambitious, and also with a finely honed sense of honor and propriety. In his second year of teaching, he put together a course in which Bellow and Howard Nemerov and John Berryman and Peter Taylor—four prizewinning, very expensive American writers in early middle age—came to teach for one week each. It was in that class that I met Phil Roth.

Yes, Roth was most imposing. He had *bearing*. He must have had it when he was ten. Tom Rogers was one of his good friends. Tom was even taller, but blond and skinny. They made an interesting pair.

A few years later, I too had become an editor. Houghton Mifflin wanted me to canvas around and read the literary magazines, and find them a few great things. While I'm in this mood of thanking Chicago, I should thank it for how easy that was.

For instance, there was Roth, with a manuscript all but finished. *Goodbye, Columbus.* Elation. Succès d'estime. Right touch of scandal. National Book Award. Then we begin to learn about life. There is a long story, funny in retrospect, about how a perfect book jacket can succumb to blunders, how an august Boston publisher can get both stodgy and huffy at the wrong time, and how a young editor looks with egg on his face. The story has nothing to do with Chicago, except perhaps to prove that a purely bookish friendship, born of a few bright remarks about texts in a writing class, can survive all kinds of moral and material damage.

At Chicago, writing was not simple for Phil. I know. I can testify. He was very much aware of alternative styles and the different questions you can ask yourself about how you're choosing to write—what stance you're taking, what voice you're using, how you shape it, how you make beginnings and endings and transitions. He was not one of those writers who, early on, accept the medium as they think they understand it—who feel, "Oh I know what it is to write"; it's just a question of "Can I get my experience down, get it out there?" Phil was many-minded about writing.

Editing *Goodbye, Columbus* was pretty easy for both of us. It was a matter of confirming his feeling that some stories were too directly an attempt to do what his father wanted—were too simply Ellis-Island-to-Hester-Street sagas of the difficulties of Jewish immigrants. You know: heartrending episodes among his parents' and his grandparents' generations as they tried to be nice to each other while exhausting themselves working and getting a nest egg together and figuring out how they could face the suburbs at the same time as they were desperate to figure out how to get there at all costs, whether they could face them or not. They were a more conventional lot than he was.

Maybe, at twenty-three, he was more egotistical-sublime than he seemed. But I don't think so. I remember some of the stories he left out of *Goodbye, Columbus.* They were imbued with a dutiful sense of what sort of ethnic song he should sing if he wanted to serve his people and serve the obvious public. He didn't have the heart for that task. He couldn't strum that lyre. So he began projecting his American Jews into unfamiliar territory, allowing them the loneliness of realizing they didn't even know their own tradition, their own past.

It's always fun to remember juvenilia. Once in a while, I recall snatches of my crummy efforts, back then at Chicago, to do a Brechtian kind of social satire about American materialism.

I remember—and shudder. But then I think, well, have I come any further in finding a better thing to say?

No, I've just taken more shots at it. And some of them have worked out.

Maybe Chicago taught me how to wait for, and recognize, good work. Even from myself. Maybe it even taught me how to blurt out something right and serviceable off the cuff, but not settle for it. Maybe it inculcated a patience with oneself: to reserve judgment until one *gets* to better judgment—to keep expecting a few late aperçus.

George Steiner

George Steiner is compact and intent; courtly, yet fierce in the persistence of his attention. And it is at once strikingly apparent that Steiner speaks, extempore, in perfect sentences: their clarity, balance, and precision provide safe passage for a tunneling intensity and intellectual restlessness.

French-born, Steiner earned a B.A. from the University of Chicago in 1947. A fiction writer, a critic, and a scholar, he is the author of the novel *The Portage to San Cristobal of A.H.* (Simon & Schuster, 1981) and the short-story collections *Anno Domini* (Simon & Schuster, 1981) and *Proofs and Three Parables* (Penguin, 1993), as well as of *The Death of Tragedy* (Hill & Wang, 1962), *Language and Silence* (Atheneum, 1967), *After Babel* (Oxford University Press, 1975), and many other works. Steiner is a fellow of Churchill College, Cambridge University, and has also taught on the faculties of the University of Geneva and Princeton. He is a regular contributor to *The New Yorker* and other journals and magazines.

GEORGE STEINER *Intellectual passions*

I'm a person who believes that sleeping is a dreadful thing, because you can't read. I've always wondered why we have to sleep so much. Sleeping seems to be a monumental waste of a third of one's life, when I haven't even begun to read or reread the books which I'm desperate to read and reread. I'm aching with the desire to read.

Yet I think the problems I have given my life to—problems of meaning, of man, of religion—are located in music more than in literature. If I could start all over again, I would be in the world of music. Having said this, the damn trouble is that you can count on the fingers of one hand the people who have had anything real to say about music. Language doesn't manage it.

I could not live, I think, without hearing music.

I heard a lot of jazz when I was a student at Chicago. Yes, yes, yes. And it was a great, great moment. At a place called the Beehive, I discovered jazz *and* Caesar salad. To this day, the two go together.

I came out of a European education, and was looking, perhaps a little arrogantly, for a chance to get my B.A. as quickly as possible. I had read about Robert Hutchins's magnificent experimental program at the University of Chicago. I was indeed able to get my B.A. in one year, and then, right away, I started graduate school at Chicago—very young, with a real chance to get going.

The university was one of the happiest, most passionate periods of my life. Chicago was, and is, an electric city, a city in which even the difficulties of daily life have a certain kind of bracing energy. I was away from home for the first time, being initiated to life; there were wonderful moments outside schooling.

I learned how to play poker, and that was a delight. I played with a circle of people at least one of whom struck me as having genius, and I mean that seriously: Hugh Hefner. He was a brilliant mind. I've never met him again.

I was taught to play by my roommate, an ex-paratrooper and a war veteran who thought I was the funniest, silliest little thing on two legs. He was quite right: here came this completely sheltered, unformed nobody. *He* was the real thing. And he was so amused by me that he decided to educate me in fundamental ways.

It was pretty rough on the South Side then. He was streetwise in the largest sense. We went everywhere. He took me to Cicero. He took me to Gary, Indiana, which was the toughest steel town in the United States. It was a wonderful education; I owe him a great deal. And, in turn, I was able to help him with his work, because I'd been intellectually so overtrained. But what he taught me was far more important than what I was able to teach him.

I've been in three university systems—European, British, and American. I've been a professor in three, and a student in three, which is rather unusual. And now that I'm in old age, almost, I look back on the Chicago experience, and it still remains unique. Hutchins had a conception whereby there were two vital moves.

One was to bring you into contact with men of immense eminence whom you didn't necessarily understand very well or even work with, but they were around. It's difficult to explain. For me, a great university is where people get an almost physical whiff of supreme quality. And that I did. For instance, when I was there, Fermi was lecturing to idiots like myself, rethinking the basis of physics— and Richard McKeon in philosophy, and Allen Tate in literature. The campus was large, and already under great economic and housing pressures. Nevertheless, there was intimacy within a large, complicated circle.

The second point: no one had to apologize for intellectual passions. The credo of my life is, you can't negotiate passions. If people don't accept them, or don't regard them as socially useful or economically valuable, they may well be right. And so you say, "I'm sorry, I am in the possession of an artistic or intellectual or scientific passion. *It* possesses *me*. It's a cancer in my soul." Hutchins said, "If that's happened to you, you're incredibly lucky, and we're going to do everything to see to it that you can develop what limited skills you have." He felt there are things that don't need to be debated.

His abrasiveness, his arrogance of intellect, his wonderful energy, his "I-can-do-anything" attitude—that was Hutchins. He had been the youngest dean of Yale's law school in American history and was one of the youngest chancellors of a major university in American history. Hutchins simply made no secret of the fact that the world was run by very able and gifted people, and that was how it had been since ancient Athens, and probably it would be until the extinction of the globe. If you worked hard enough, and if you exercised a passionate discipline, you might be able to join that club in one way or another. The doors to the club were open. But you had to work very, very hard to get in.

All around the campus were people without our privileges, people who hadn't had our chances, who could only work in the evening, who were sitting around tables with some of the men who taught us, reading Plato and Aristotle and Locke and Hobbes. I felt incredibly privileged and lucky that I could do this fulltime, and I also had the sense of a continuum—that the books were out there in the city. Hutchins had that vision.

He was totally unembarrassed about excellence—a marvelous thing. If you could do better than anyone else, go for it, try for it. No one was more excited about modern times, about political changes, but he linked them, always, with the high tradition of classical, medieval, and Renaissance scholarship. Many men are great traditionalists; many men are great modernists. But to put them together in a way that was not artificial is very rare. He wired them up; I can use no other image. The current came through both ways. He lived the continuity as few human beings have done. The continuity and the novelty: it flowed naturally. For me that was Chicago's distinctive strength.

The university was immensely liberating for those who wanted to work very hard, depressing for those who didn't. It was not a place in which you could just have a good time. First, the climate was too harsh. Second, you were encouraged to go fast. Hutchins despised holidays, despised breaks. He was a workaholic, and no one was ashamed of trying to be one after him. He hated sloppiness, mediocrity, cowardice; he made no secret of his standards. He made bitter enemies because of this. If you weren't up to it, get out. No bluffing. And as he was very, very demanding of himself, he didn't see why he shouldn't be demanding of others. Hutchins was a high Platonic elitist, through and through.

He was from an old Puritan New England background, yet Hutchins had a welcoming generosity toward the Babel of human tongues. Languages excite me profoundly. When I hear one I don't know, I have an almost animal ache to start learning it. And at Chicago, at that time, there was a tremendous variety. The other European refugee students with me were from everywhere. There was a lot of Russian around. The university was beginning to get geniuses out of Asia. The accents I heard among teachers were rich and comforting.

Hutchins was also very welcoming to Jewish scholars. The university had the greatest living Jewish thinker, Leo Strauss, and Bruno Bettelheim, whom I worked with down the road. Chicago had a brilliant Jewish community. But in some ways it was provincial. It did not have the New York pressures; it did not have the great feuds. People were not caught up in the New York fever. They were doing much more important work. They blended into a certain American optimism.

The full news of the Holocaust wouldn't impinge until some years later. It looked as if Hitler had been well and truly beaten, and as if American horizons for Jews were unlimited—as they were. All the doors were opening. So I met something I hadn't met in the tragic European situation—a *confident* intellectual Judaism. That was a great discovery.

Having come from a pure French classical lycée tradition, in my entrance examinations I failed chemistry, physics, math, and then one thing I'd never heard of—social science. So I had to take it. It re-educated me fundamentally. I loved doing it. It was entirely fresh to me, and beautifully taught. It was a revelation! I was like a monk coming out onto Broadway. There was a rushing world out there of science and social studies, and though of course I didn't go in those directions, I'm eternally grateful for the training I got.

I discovered great science writing. Hutchins had instituted a course whereby you read philosophic, legal, and scientific texts, and suddenly I realized they were marvelously written. Now, that may seem silly. It isn't. If you've been brought up on European literature, and Latin and Greek, or even in the more conservative American tradition, you never read a page of Darwin or Newton or the Dred Scott decision or Keynes. A fantastic idea—to show you that great prose, great thought, is part of the history of the language, whether it argues about evolution or American slavery or economics. Hutchins insisted that you combat texts outside your natural specialty.

Another wonderful thing: I wasn't forced to choose a

major. They said, "If you aren't sure, find out." And I didn't know. Should it be literature or philosophy? So I did both, heavily.

I studied with Allen Tate and Richard McKeon. I must have learned a great deal from the techniques of my teachers, but probably subconsciously. You couldn't have found two more different men: the poet and Southern essayist, complicated and shy and wonderful Tate; and the great, robust McKeon, already a member of UNESCO, a representative of America in European culture, a Thomist. The contrast was marvelous; working closely with them was to see both worlds.

As a matter of fact, to this day I haven't chosen between those worlds. That indecision has stayed with me. My teaching is both in philosophy and in literature. If I had to define what I do in Geneva and other places, it's where philosophy and literature meet. Tate tried to encourage me to become a writer, McKeon a scholar. I've tried to keep both very much alive within me.

I was writing poetry (which I submitted to Tate) until the wonderful day when I stared at the damn stuff and said, "This is very good verse—and there's nothing worse." Verse is about a million light-years from poetry. The difference between poetry and verse: verse is something you can do by skill, by education, by having read a great deal. Poetry is a very different animal. It's so different it's embarrassing.

I'm not good enough to be a great creator, and what distinguishes me from my academic colleagues is that I know it and say it, and they don't—which is a big difference.

A real creator—we don't know how that comes about. One doesn't choose. I didn't choose! The genetics of it are unknown to us. The neurophysiology of a great musician, a great painter, is certainly unknown to us. As a critic, what I do—and it's worth doing—is, I carry the mail. I am given letters and told, "You find the right mailbox." Sometimes I'm allowed to carry the mail—new art, new literature—and put it in the mailbox, and say, "Please read this." Finding the right mailbox isn't always easy. It's an immense privilege. One must never confuse it with having written the letter.

Already, younger, I knew that the kind of brain powers I had—which could take exams, which could pick up new languages, which could analyze—were not those of the artist. There is in the artist a great innocence. There is in the artist an immediacy that I do not have.

There is in the real creator, sometimes, a wonderful vanity. It protects him from insight. It makes him take the big risks. When I meet young poets and novelists who figure they're the hottest thing that's ever happened, I envy them deeply, because that error may make it possible for them to create their work.

I drew and painted a lot; I wrote a lot of verse. If I did have possibilities, they may have been diminished by the power of my French education and my Chicago education, which of course opted for analytic, intellectual, argumentative powers.

I have published a good deal of fiction. I've at least had the joy of keeping my hand in, in a very marginal way. So it hasn't been all sadness. But I tell my students, "Never mix up the two." And that avoids a lot of waste.

From Tate I learned to make twenty drafts when I thought fifteen were more than enough. I learned a kind of scruple of elegance and perfection which I learned again, later, from Mr. Shawn at the *New Yorker*. Having Shawn edit me was very much like having Allen Tate. They had the same wonderful caring for detail. Tate also made me feel, in my bones, that even the most pure of lyric poems is a deeply political act. I learned from him that there is no such thing as a poem outside of human conflict.

The place was full of brilliant young writers. I met a number of poets who went on to write real poetry. And the Committee on Social Thought of the University of Chicago said, "Okay, if you're a novelist, come in, and if you're Hannah Arendt come in, and if you're Ed Shils . . ." (Shils, too, didn't distinguish between literature and philosophical argument.) So it was the right climate.

Hutchins had a terrific social-political engagement, a sense that he had to get things done within a system, and that the real masters who change history know how to work with committees they despise.

I'm much more European—a loner, a mandarin. I rejected Hutchins's final commitment to the sociological and social process, and I may have been very wrong in doing so.

But you can't be everything, and you can't fake it. You have to try to come home to yourself. My training and deep conviction are that no committee has ever done a goddamn thing worth doing *since* the one that wrote the Old Testament.

On the whole, I'm a human being who, when he enters a room and starts agreeing with somebody, is greatly worried. I've been a nomad. I wanted to be.

A poet has to be rooted. I teach in Italian, French, German, and English—and live in them. A poet has to be at home within a tongue, has to have a sleepwalker's singleness of identification with it. That is not my case.

Richard Stern

Richard Stern has taught at the University of Chicago since 1955. He earned a B.A. from the University of North Carolina (1947), an M.A. from Harvard (1949), and a Ph.D. from the University of Iowa (1954).

His novels include *Golk* (Criterion, 1960), *Stitch* (Harper & Row, 1965), *Other Men's Daughters* (Dutton, 1973), *Natural Shocks* (Coward, 1978) and *A Father's Words* (Arbor House, 1986). Among his collections of fiction are *Packages* (Coward, 1980), *Noble Rot: Stories 1949–1988* (Grove, 1989), and *Shares and Other Fictions* (Delphinium, 1992).

As a longtime member of the university community, Stern knows the place better than most. Some of his fiction has been set there, taking the measure of people like and unlike himself.

RICHARD STERN *Tenacity*

My parents had a big dictionary. Perhaps because they'd spent so much money on it, they felt it should be used. So I got in the habit of looking up words.

I would look up the word, then encounter it three or four times in the next days. I can remember looking the same word up so often that I began to doubt my ability to remember anything at all.

My father invented stories for us. My first memory is of sighting him through the slats of my crib as he told my sister and me stories.

He told us about a midget lady named Miss Demicapoulos, who had extraordinary adventures. He made up wonderful names, some of which I've used in my fiction. The stories were funny, tragic, enthralling.

He must have gotten a kick out of making them up, but he never wrote anything until he retired at seventy-eight, and I bought him a little notebook, insisting that he write an autobiography. My sister and I had it printed. It's a brief, charming, heartrending memoir about the family and his experiences as a dentist in New York.

At some point, one becomes this thing called a writer. It happened to me when I was twelve.

I had to write a story for class. Already I was reading a lot and had written sketches; my story was more or less pilfered from something I'd read. I had the gratification of laughter from the class and approval from the teacher. I'd never before had an audience of more than my father and mother.

As a boy, I went to summer camp and performed in plays. I was considered a pretty good actor. I enjoyed that, but it didn't bring the gratification writing did. The nicest thing about acting was the ensemble work. Part of that involves watching other people act.

Writing came from *me*, even when—as I've said—it was half-stolen.

There's the pleasure of being by oneself, being able to think about *anything*, feeling that this is a justified part of life, not being told, "You're daydreaming. Get with it."

Daydreaming is what you do.

Then you have to get it down; with luck, it—writing—begets itself.

If I have a recognizable voice in fiction, it's a voice of parsimony, economy, omission—a certain obliquity and sharpness. I seldom get that in a first draft. The first draft is rather pompous, the syntax winding around as I'm trying to encompass the action.

I found a paper of mine that I'd written at seventeen at Chapel Hill on philosophy. It was just two pages on Aristotle, and it was written in the same sort of tight way that I write now. So I must have had a certain gift for concision. I've allied it to something I hated in my mother. After I'd read a Karen Horney book in 1947, I called it anality. It was her obsession with cleanliness. I think it's been transformed by me into a finicky style.

What's easy for me—maybe it's connected to my old theatrical interest—is talking "for" other people, for my characters. I can talk in different ways pretty easily.

There's also the question of breath. Isaac Babel said his sentences were short because he had asthma. (Of course, Proust had asthma, too.) Still, I think there's some relationship between a person's physical being and his work.

I haven't analyzed it, but I know that after a certain time, I get tired, yet I know I'd be better off if I developed scenes more, let the characters bang each other around more than I do. I tend to edit sharply, narrowly, around the key signatures.

In the last ten years, my working method has been that of dictating to an assistant. His—or her—reaction is important. Does he or she laugh? Does he or she seem to tune out? Attentiveness is important. It means one person cares. At times, I've felt that nobody cared; sometimes I didn't care myself.

Writing doesn't get easier.

This year I came out of a writing slump. I had been ready to throw in the towel. (I had begun to feel that way as well about some of my fellow writers. I thought they too should throw in the towel.) But I recovered from surgery, went back to teaching, and started up again.

On the whole, the university has been a good place for me. I came here in 1955 after a year teaching at a small college for women in New London, Connecticut.

I had read about Chicago in a *Life* magazine article that called it "the greatest university that's ever been." (Henry Luce did lots of PR for Hutchins.) When I came here, I was impressed by it, and with myself for being part of it. I was writing a novel, *Europe,* and stories at the time; I was writing a lot.

Norman Maclean was very helpful to me. He saw to it that I had mornings free to write; I taught in the afternoons.

Maclean was fascinating both for the power and the self-cancellation of power in him—for his authenticity and for his romantic elaboration of it. The clash between his complex feelings and his romantic, Hemingway-and-Western image puzzled him—baffled him. Introspection worried him. He did not analyze his character, did not work out the clash between his nature and his romantic view of what a man should be. The sensitive "tough guy" is a tough role. There was much more to him than that. He believed in discipline, but he didn't know how to discipline or use his own feelings. His wonderful wife, Jessie, tightened that emotional knot; she was a purer "Westerner" than he.

An amazing thing happened after he was free of the theatrical tension of teaching. He'd been a part of a critical circle, the Chicago School, headed by R. S. Crane and McKeon, the philosopher. What distinguished them was critical ferocity. I think Norman took a beating there. When he was free of that, too, he wrote down some family stories he had told for years, *A River Runs Through It*.

The great thing about the university is the remarkable people in all fields. I've been lucky to know a couple of hundred marvelous men and women here. I've spent a lot of time listening to them, having all sorts of things explained.

The danger of teaching is that knowing things students don't yet know evokes their gratitude and amazement. You can get drunk on that. As a writer, you have to address an audience that can't be so easily amazed and delighted. You're not in a cozy apartment but on the frontier. Very different stuff.

It's been important for me to get away from the university from time to time. I wanted to get around the world, be at home everywhere. I have managed to see a bit, maybe too much, but I've loved the charged anonymity of travel.

One way in which I came to know Chicago involved a controversy surrounding the *Chicago Review* in 1958 or 1959. I had been made chairman of its faculty committee.

The *Review* had an editor who was a friend of the San Francisco writers, Ginsberg, Burroughs, et al. He started publishing them, quite a coup. *Naked Lunch* appeared in the magazine. Meanwhile, some of the students on the magazine were telling me that other manuscripts were coming in and weren't being considered for publication, just rejected out of hand.

Such complaints were made before an obscenity controversy erupted. A columnist named Jack Mabley published a piece in the *Chicago Daily News* which said the *Review* was publishing obscene material. (He and the paper were on an obscenity kick.) That in itself didn't create much of a stir, but as I was to learn from the university's president, Lawrence Kimpton, Mayor Daley was being pressured about the matter by certain prominent Catholics in the city.

Daley told Kimpton—*he* told me—"I've been trying to get the City Council to pass such and such an ordinance to save the university in Hyde Park." Hyde Park was in decay. If it continued, the university would be endangered. Daley believed the university was essential to a great Chicago.

The ordinances had to do with squeezing the criminal and slum-landlord element out. Cardinal Stritch had recently died, and there was a power fight in the Church. Many of the people who were squeezed out of Hyde Park moved to the area called Back of the Yards. The priest there used the *Review*'s supposed obscenity to attack the university in his diocesan paper. Daley told Kimpton that the Church was putting pressure on Catholic council members, whose votes he needed. Kimpton's initial reaction was to suppress the *Review*, cancel it. We committee members met with him in his office and when he told us this, we said, "Are you kidding? Censor the *Chicago Review*? You'd degrade the university. You can't do it." Kimpton saw that immediately and drew back.

Meanwhile, a couple of the *Review* editors saw an opportunity in the situation. They wrote about it to John Ciardi at the *Saturday Review*, who wrote a column, most of it wrong. The issue became a great debate, some of which is recorded in many issues of the *Chicago Maroon*. My position was that everything accepted by the editors had to be printed by the *Review*. Instead, the editors took the pieces to start another magazine, *Big Table*. They staged a benefit to raise money for it. (I appeared at the benefit and read a story that *Big Table* printed.)

There are still people who think the *Chicago Review* was "suppressed." It's a myth, but a useful one to remind people that literature can easily become the casualty of other interests.

I learned a lot from the whole experience. It was amazing to me that a power fight in the Church could reach the City Council and that in turn could affect the university. I also learned a bit about publicity and the distortions of claims along such sensational lines as "literary martyrdom." By chance, I was reading at the time a book called *The Montesi Affair* by Wayland Young. It was about what happened in Italy after someone misheard a conversation in a restaurant about the drowning of a girl named Montesi. The misunderstanding became a rumor that nearly overthrew the Italian government. The *Chicago Review* was my Montesi affair.

I had just started work on my Ph.D. at Iowa in 1952 when John Crowe Ransom wrote that he'd accepted a story of mine for the *Kenyon Review*. That wonderful moment when you're suddenly part of the makers of literature! I suppose that pleasure is connected to the pleasure I've had meeting Thomas Mann, Ezra Pound, and Samuel Beckett, the feeling that you're connected to those who've formed your mind and helped make your life comprehensible, moving, lighter, deeper.

I differentiate this acquaintance from friendships with such men as Bellow and Roth. Their work has meant even more to me, but they are part of what Roth called "my life as a man." Actually Beckett, too, I regarded as a friend. Though I saw him only eight or nine times, I spoke intimately with him. When he spoke about Joyce, I felt the mental marble dissolve. When he praised Bellow's work and something of mine, I felt the literary earth shake, as if Sophocles or Chaucer had acknowledged me and my pals.

I try to tell my students, particularly my writing students, that they can be part of this linkage, that, in a way, through this minor connection in front of them, they're already part of it. It's important at the University of Chicago, where the Great Books loom monumentally, to free students from the paralysis of being intimidated. I don't hesitate to compare the best student work with the work of masters. This is not meant to cheapen the marvelous, but to evoke it. The hope is to make students fall in love with sublimity and to show them it's not out of reach.

There's a lot of brilliance, even genius, around, but between flashes of genius and careers of accomplishment are pitfalls of life and character. To be an artist you need luck and tenacity, terrific tenacity. Maybe the obstacles to art exist to warn off those who can't bear the pain of creative exhaustion, misunderstanding, devaluation—or devastatingly accurate evaluation—self-exposure, critical wounds, many other things. It's a long trip from the stories coming through the slats of a crib to those you have to get down on paper sixty-odd years later.

Nathaniel Tarn

French-born Nathaniel Tarn, an anthropologist, a poet, and a translator, attended the University of Chicago as a Smith-Mundt/Fulbright fellow in anthropology in 1952.

He has taught at the universities of Chicago and London, among others. He was founder and director of the Cape Goliard Press at Jonathan Cape, and founding general editor of Cape Editions.

His poetry collections include *Old Savage/Young City* (Random, 1965); *The Beautiful Contradictions* (Random, 1970); *A Nowhere for Vallejo* (Random, 1971); *Lyrics for the Bride of God* (New Directions, 1975); *The House of Leaves* (Black Sparrow Press, 1976); *Atitlan/Alashka* (Small Press Distribution, 1979); and *Seeing America First* (Coffee House Press, 1989). Tarn's translations include *The Heights of Macchu Picchu* (Farrar, Straus & Giroux, 1967) and *Selected Poems* (Delacorte, 1972), both by Neruda. Tarn's *Views from the Weaving Mountain: Selected Essays in Poetry and Anthropology* was published by the University of New Mexico in 1991.

Tarn is now an American citizen and lives near Santa Fe, New Mexico. A rangy, vigorous man, he offers paradoxes with enthusiastic confidence. His laughter often buffets authority, and so do his words.

NATHANIEL TARN *Poetry and anthropology*

How do you lead a life in poetry? Sometimes, if you're lucky, you're thrown or born into it; you have no alternative *but* that life. Yet in other cases, life may involve the acquisition of another profession. In my case, anthropology allowed me to lead a life before I became a poet.

I was in a curious position. I was born in France in 1928 and brought up in French-speaking territory. I went to England because of the war (my father was British), and so had several years of British education, including Cambridge. But I never felt at home in England. After Cambridge, I had this very romantic notion that I would go back to Paris, get back to my roots, write in French—and thus condemned myself to years of agony.

A knowledge of other languages automatically opens up other mental structures, because you can say certain things in one language that you cannot in another. But the bilingual situation for a poet is a nightmare. It's wonderful for everybody *except* the poet. Unless you decide to write in two languages, which is extremely difficult for a poet, you go through hell trying to decide which language to write in.

It's a commonplace that French is a very, very intellectual language. It's a wonderful language for intellectuals. It's a magnificent poetic language, too, but I have always felt it to be very constrictive.

It's difficult to *invent* in French; it's difficult to get out of certain mental sets. If you're writing in French, you're always being pushed toward the more intellectual side of things, whereas English has always had an enormous nonintellectual dimension, as well as the intellectual one. English is a much broader language. For me, English was in some ways a liberation.

At any rate, after finishing at Cambridge, I fiddled about with a bit of journalism in Paris. I was constantly being pressed, particularly by my parents, to get a "respectable job," poetry being nothing but a "hobby." And I didn't know what job I wanted.

Then one day, I saw a movie, and in the movie were pictures of the Musée de l'Homme, the big anthropological museum in Paris. I said to myself, "My God, I've never seen this!" So I went there. The Museum of Man, as it was called, had a very large and attractive display of anthropological specimens, "primitive art," and so on.

I'd been attracted to anthropology for some time through my general reading, but hadn't systematized the interest. To cut a long story short, three days later I started a career as an anthropologist, enrolling at the Musée as an anthropology student. I studied there for two years before going on to win a Smith-Mundt/Fulbright fellowship to study anthropology under Robert Redfield at the University of Chicago from 1951 to 1952. Just after that, Redfield sent me to do doctoral fieldwork in Guatemala.

How has my career as an anthropologist fed my life as a poet? In some ways, that's like asking what life is like outside a certain skin and what life is like inside a certain skin. The only thing you know about is *inside* the skin.

Anthropology, at its most basic, gave me a bridge, gave me something valuable to do while I was finding my way in what would eventually become my main preoccupation— poetry. Anthropology kept me busy while other things were being sorted out.

At the time when I was an anthropology student, my fate, as it were, was undetermined. I had not yet decided whether to write in French or in English. I was also playing with the idea of being a visual artist (I had been a serious painter and had won a bunch of prizes). But anthropology gave me a craft and a point of view on the world that I've never really lost.

I think anybody who reads my poetry will see that anthropology has contributed a great deal to it. To begin with, anthropology got me interested in religion and philosophy, belief systems, ritual systems, symbolic systems—in myth and in the huge edifice of thought around myth. Myths are in my poetry all the time, particularly the constitutive myth of lyric, which is the Orphic complex: Orpheus, Persephone, Eurydice, and so on. And quite frequently the mode of thinking in my work is influenced by the slightly removed, somewhat objective, at times fairly ironic, analytical approach to phenomena encouraged at that time.

Even the terminology of anthropology comes in sometimes. Not that anthropology's vocabulary is as rich as, for instance, the vocabulary of sailing would be, or printing, or pottery, all of which are older vocabularies, and all of which are linked directly to matter: pottery to clay, sailing to wood and the conditions of the sea. Languages arise most fruitfully from wholly material things. And anthropology is not linked to matter; it's mental stuff. You also reach, very fast, a limit in the anthropological terminology you can use in poetry that general readers will recognize. Most of it, indeed, is not very "poetic."

But still, if anybody were to do a serious study of my work, they would probably find the connections between the poetry and the anthropology pretty clear. It's not just the myths that are present, but the personae.

The personae get in there very early. My first book, *Old Savage/Young City,* offers an ironical take on anthropology. The title poem is about an old Amerindian chief who comes to what is fairly obviously New York City and looks at the white culture, thinking about what it means for *his* culture—mainly destruction, of course. In *The Beautiful Contradictions* there are even two long sections on my doctoral experience in Guatemala.

Anthropology really has informed my poetry, both in a theoretical way and in the poetry's content, as much as anything possibly could.

At the Musée, I quickly found out that 90 percent of anthropology was Anglo-Saxon, either English or American. So the logical thing to do was to study in England or America. On my fellowship application, I was asked to list three universities where I would like to study. Chicago was one of my three, because it had a world reputation for anthropology.

So I duly sailed to America on an ocean liner. I got to New York and was astonished—particularly by the number of windows you can look out at from certain other windows. I was staying with friends in a huge apartment block, and when I looked out, I could see fifty or sixty people doing their thing opposite. That was wild.

Next was this appalling business of so-called orientation. You were not really deemed, in those days, to have lived seriously until you hit American shores. You had to have an "orientation"; you had to understand American *democracy*, because Europe, basically, was not democratic. I was told that!

And you had to have a lot of *problems*. This was the great age of Freud in America, and you had to have problems! Adaptation problems, all sorts of problems. And I just didn't *have* any. As far as I was concerned, the minute I hit New York, I was on home ground.

I was mildly annoyed that we were sent to Yale for orientation. I had hoped, having had a unisex education up to that point, that I'd go to a nice coed university and have myself a little fun. No way! At Yale one night, they actually imported thirty nurses from some hospital to dance with the foreign students. You know, Jesus! It was awfully stilted!

It was with some relief that I finally got to Chicago. I was assigned to International House, which I immediately found unnerving. It was a dormitory situation, and the sexes were rigorously segregated. There was a men's wing, and there was a women's wing. I seem to remember that women could visit the men's side once a year. I can't imagine it *was* as bad as that, but I have a feeling that it was.

I got out of International House quickly. I was there with another young French guy, Claude Tardits, who's since become an eminent Africanist in Paris, and we formed a kind of couple, because in those days, if you weren't married or going steady, you didn't fit in socially. Everything went two by two.

I remember the process of registration. It was incredibly strange to us, because here was this huge hall, and all the professors, all the departments had their tables, and you would file in and have brief talks with people. It looked like joining the army, because of the size of the place, though there actually was some personal contact. We were recognized as special, in the sense that we were Smith-Mundt/Fulbright fellowship holders. Fred Eggan was at the anthropology table. He was a very kind man, wonderful to us.

And then began my frenzied year at the University of Chicago.

Robert Redfield took me on as one of his boys. I was in a difficult position, because my education had been interrupted. For some reason, Eggan and Redfield seemed to think that Claude and I had been incredibly well educated in France: there was such respect for Lévi-Strauss and various others. But in fact, French anthropological education was not an enormous deal. It was very French—there were hundreds of things which simply were not covered at all. Redfield could probably not have evolved his school of anthropology had he passed through a system like the French one, which gave primacy in education to philosophy. Redfield's anthropology raised philosophical questions, which in France probably would have been relegated to a philosophy department, not to an anthropology department. (When Redfield gave lectures in Paris, they met with a very mixed reception.) Philosophical matters might never have been raised in anthropology at Chicago if people there had had the same grounding as the French or had shared a firmly established international tradition.

So in fact we were infinitely more ignorant than we were taken for. And we kept on going to the professors and confessing, trying to say, "Hey, you know, are you really sure we can do this?" Because what we were doing, basically, was the Ph.D. prep in one year. (Normally, it takes two or three years.) Apart from the French stuff, we didn't know anything.

We were working and working and working and working.

Encountering American professors was a far more open experience than encountering English professors or French professors had been. I mean, God, I worked for three years with Lévi-Strauss, and I think we may have exchanged fifteen words in those three years. You just didn't *talk* to your professors in Europe!

The Chicago professors were open, but not completely so. I remember feeling that there was something somewhat Olympian about them. With Redfield, for example, I didn't have much of a personal relation, although I saw him every week at our seminar.

Redfield was perhaps the most Olympian of them all. I used to think of him as a cross between an eighteenth-century English country gentleman and an American pioneer, but with the gentleman very much in the ascendant.

I only went to his house once. He drove me there. I remember that he was going along these six-lane highways, which always daunted and amazed me, because we didn't have such things in Europe. He was bombing along with the greatest of ease. I asked him, "Aren't you terrified?"

"Oh, no," Redfield replied. "I just love driving back and forth. It's great relaxation."

Later, in correspondence when I was in Guatemala, he was very supportive. He was much more personal in the correspondence than he'd ever been in person.

I was closer to Fred Eggan, who was liable to be more friendly in a pat-on-the-back basis than Redfield was. Sol Tax was also a friend, but my work and his were not connected, so I didn't get to know him really well.

Subsequently Eggan retired to New Mexico; I read a poem at his memorial service six months ago. Redfield I last saw in London at a lunch or tea in about 1955 or 1956. I believe that the leukemia had already set in.

At Chicago, professional distance was emphasized by the visit of Paul Radin to the university. Paul was very informal with his students, very close and friendly at all times. He was a peripatetic visiting professor, because I don't think anybody, anywhere, wanted to give him a permanent job. He was a difficult character, in the sense that he sent a lot of shots across the bows of the establishment.

Radin used to say, "Well, you know, this American food is all very well, but if I can eat with *Europeans*. . ." So he would turn up at the apartment where Tardits and I lived, with a package of meat and stuff under his arm, and demand that we cook it. He was an incredible storyteller, and had an immense fund of gossip and good information to draw on. He was great fun. But the problem was that we couldn't do our homework!

Was I writing? Yes and no. I was in a very difficult position, because I was making that transfer from French to English. I had not yet decided what I was going to do after Chicago; as far as I knew, I was going to go back to France.

But it was beginning to dawn on me that since I'd never

written anything satisfactory in French—for some reason, I couldn't get it off the ground—maybe English was, after all, my language. I'd never published anything. Everything was still in notebooks.

I probably wrote a few poems—in French. I kept my diary. (My diary's been going since 1939. In those days, it was still in French.) But I had no literary contacts whatsoever. We were just too busy in anthro; we had to keep our noses to the grindstone. Even if I'd wanted to contact the English department and found out what was going on, I simply wouldn't have had the time or energy.

I don't remember any literary readings. There probably were some. There was probably a magazine; I don't remember it. (Years later, I published quite a bit in the *Chicago Review*.) If I'd pushed, I could have gotten some introductions to people in the English department, but this simply didn't occur. I was so determined to be a good anthropologist that I'm not sure there was even time to read literature. We were at it eighteen hours a day.

If I had known about such things, there were a lot of experimental literary activities going on in America at that time, like the Beats and Black Mountain, which presumably I could have leapt into when I left Chicago. If not for anthropology, I could have gone to Black Mountain College! But these literary experiments were very small, known to only a few people. Since I didn't have any contact with writers at all—not *at all;* nowhere, nowhere, nowhere!—how could I have known?

I managed to get some literary reading done when I was in the field in Guatemala, just after Chicago, having been sent there by Redfield. I remember sitting between two candles in a village that had no electricity, reading *Ulysses,* which I'd taken down with me. But not in Chicago.

Both Claude and I got to be very fond of the university. Yet we did find the good, gray Gothic rather forbidding.

I think particularly when you're young, it's usually the people you're fond of, over the place, unless the place is either so paradisal or so intolerable that it really obtrudes.

Of the graduate students I knew at Chicago, all of us are still friends, and some I'm actually still in touch with, which I think says something for the quality of the relationships. As I've mentioned, it was an exceedingly busy time. We were working like dogs, so the fact that there was any social life at all is rather miraculous.

There wasn't much, and what there was struck me as warm, but bizarre. Claude and I would be invited to some party by a fellow student. We'd get to the top of the stairs, knock on the door, door would open, we'd walk in, can of beer shoved into our hands, sit down in front of the television, and watch a boxing match or a football match. And this was it! *This* was it! I couldn't believe it. It's probably the only time in my life that I've watched sports.

At our own parties, a student from the English department would usually show up and play his guitar, and I was always asked to sing with him. I would sing a French medieval song.

I never even really saw the city of Chicago until right at the very end. Only in the last fifteen or twenty days of that year did I get out into the city. Redfield had decided to send me to Guatemala, so I had to buy field equipment, clothes, and this, that, and the other.

There was one exception: Claude and I used to go to hear jazz a lot, sometimes in the black jazz clubs; we'd be the only white people there. And we went quite far into black churches and anywhere that would have good singing, the ritual singing, and possessions and trances. Claude and I were completely fascinated. It's the only time in my life that I've seen jazz in context. There it was, being made.

The trances we saw in the churches were extraordinary. We felt we were getting very close to something so fundamentally American that, in some strange way, most of American culture was trying to hide it from us. I just enjoyed the beauty of it—the singing, the community feeling, and all sorts of things which I didn't feel were present in the white world.

Our closeness to the black population was marked. In the last Chicago apartment I lived in, I could be lying on my bed in a very small bedroom, open the window, stretch my hand out, and virtually touch the bed of a black couple living next door. The street right alongside ours was almost completely black.

I remember being extraordinarily impressed by the beauty of black people: they dressed so fantastically well, seemed so extraordinarily alive in all sorts of ways. I don't think that was the anthropologist in me; it was just the visual excitement of this phenomenon. There was a wonderful feeling of physical (if not social) proximity between blacks and whites which, I gather, disappeared later, because the university got in the middle of a very difficult ethnic situation. I don't think that what we experienced in the richness of that proximity was possible to experience five or ten years after.

While at Chicago, I also got to know Northwestern. The ostensible reason was that Mel Herskovits, a major Africanist and a theoretical anthropologist, was teaching there. Claude wanted to go to his lectures. So I went with him, and we soon discovered that this was the ideal American university of our dreams. Namely, it was bright, and it was sassy. There was a lot of ice cream, and there were a lot of pretty ladies who were not all dressed up in gray Gothic. We enjoyed this. Visiting Northwestern also led me to meet the anthropologist William Bascom, which in turn took me to Cuba and led to an involvement with Afro-American work.

Our own university was not, physically speaking,

enormously attractive, but it had some fabulous features. The University of Chicago Library, for example, was a great library, always a joy to work in.

Chicago offered a fine, very fine education. I never for a minute had any doubt that going to Chicago meant going to *the* top university for anthropology at the time. It was obviously one of the intellectual powerhouses in America.

My greatest regret in life, from a professional point of view, is that the Fulbright rules stipulated that I had to go back to "my own" country after a year. It would have been far better for me if I'd stayed in the U.S., if I'd just simply stayed and not gone back.

From the first day I got to New York, I felt at home. And that feeling of home persisted. This was a country in which I was comfortable, for all sorts of reasons.

One of the reasons was that the U.S. was manifestly a country of immigrants; it was manifestly a country which you could choose. It's very difficult to *choose* to be a Britisher. It's very difficult to *choose* to be a Frenchman. But it's very natural to choose to be an American; that's what people have been doing since the eighteenth century.

I remember feeling both attracted and irritated by the extraordinary openness of American culture. On the one hand, the fact that American students always seemed to begin at the beginning, over and over again, was tiring. In schools in France you put one brick on top of another, and then you put another brick on top, and you gradually built a house—and, by and large, those walls stayed up. Whereas in America, no sooner had you put up a brick than you took it down, because you kept asking the first questions over and over.

That was exasperating, because I liked to build. Yet it was exhilarating, because nothing was taken for granted—or at least, so it seemed at the time. Obviously, once you get used to this culture, there's a lot of stuff that's taken for granted, as there is everywhere else.

I reacted very favorably to the Middle West, although I haven't chosen to live there. The houses were spacious, solid, set on huge boulevards. Hospitality was of a kind that you don't find on the coasts anymore. There's a level of comfort and ease in the Middle West. In those days, I felt that the region had two elements: comfort and space. The spaciousness was incredible and appealing. It linked up with the idea of Olsonian space, which I immediately recognized as fundamental when I read Charles Olson several years later. After an experience like that, Europe seemed extremely narrow, whatever its virtues.

For a good ten years before I actually emigrated to America in 1970, I had been interested almost exclusively in what was going on in poetry in America, not in what was going on in England. I had to pay attention to some of the English stuff, because I was working there as founding editor and director of Cape Editions and creator of Cape Goliard Press at Jonathan Cape. My professional situation demanded that I "discover" a few English titles now and then. (Besides, I was seeing those guys every day.) But the overwhelming thrust of the books I was editing and publishing at Cape in the sixties in England—95 percent or more—was American.

A critic remarked two or three years ago that in that era, the fate of American avant-garde publishing indeed rested in British, not American, hands. The most dramatic example is the fact of my publishing Charles Olson. Not just Olson, of course—there were also Zukofsky, Duncan, and many others. But Cape held the copyright on Olson for ten or fifteen years before he was eventually repatriated to this country and published by the University of California Press. That's pretty dramatic.

Possibly there may have been even more involved in the pull of America on me than all of this suggests. For instance, when I was a child in London during the blitz, I found and eagerly read a biography of Abraham Lincoln. During the bombings, I was always fantasizing about being evacuated to America, which was an actual possibility. And then there's the fact that half my family *is* American, though I've never known them well.

When the family left Europe, half of it went to England and the other half to America. My father and the Shuberts of Broadway were thus first cousins, and I've often thought how convenient it would have been if I'd been born a Shubert, instead. I would have had not only an American adulthood, but an American childhood.

But that, of course, didn't happen.

The ongoing nature of my commitment to America has kept me here. If you're interested in having any kind of audience at all as a poet, you cannot be in twenty different places at the same time; it's already difficult enough to build up an audience in *one*. And since the question of identity is still very much associated with locality and nationality, it follows automatically that I stay. Plus, I've made my life here. I wanted to go and live in the Southwest, and I went and lived there; there was no other Southwest available, that I knew of.

The only literature professorships I've ever held were in America (before that, I had taught anthropology exclusively). I married an American. It all mounts up.

People talk about Pound going to Europe and becoming European and about Eliot going to England and becoming British. But there's been a lot of movement in the opposite direction, too. There's D. H. Lawrence, a man who was technically British, and considered a British novelist, but whom I consider to be a great American poet, on the grounds that his poems do not fit one bit into the British aesthetic. (And then, of course, there are his American literature essays, which are absolutely stunning.) Lawrence came from England to *America*. And there've also been people who came to America but later returned to where they had come from. Auden came here, but never became an American poet—and went back to Oxford to die.

I do *not* think that I shall go back to Cambridge to die! One never knows, but I just don't think it's gonna happen.

If you're going to have a major education, you've gotta have a major education. There's no two ways about it. You can't spend your life shouting that you're a major university if you're a kindergarten, which a lot of them do in the U.S.

The fact of the matter is that intellectuals are technicians like other technicians, and if you're going to prepare intellectuals, they've got to be prepared in a certain way. By intellectuals, I mean minds at work, at large.

Poets are technicians of the sacred: that is Jerome Rothenberg's formulation. Poets are technicians of the word. Rothenberg opened up the relationship between poetry and anthropology in what he calls ethnopoetics. He claims to have coined that term, but I'm not absolutely certain that *I* might not have invented it while I was compiling a bibliography for Redfield at Chicago. At any rate, Rothenberg made a great contribution in linking up the primitivistic element in twentieth-century poetry to the tribal stuff produced by sages, prophets, shamans, and so on. Opening up the field that way was very liberating for many of us.

Now, you would think that having said that poets are technicians, I would then say, "All right, they need a technical education." And I don't see any harm in that particular education. If there is a place where people can be taught the rudiments of poetic writing, all the things which have been associated with it for two thousand years—fine. But I have a very dim view of the gigantic creative writing industry which has grown up in the States, mostly after I was at Chicago.

In the first place, I'm not even sure that the creative

writing schools offer fundamentals. Second, they are basically places where the teacher holds hands with the students and the students hold hands with the teacher. Various cliques and in-groups are made which last, very often, for life. And an establishment is created which has, to my mind, absolutely nothing to do with genuine poetry and everything to do with bureaucracy and other sociological mechanisms of that type. So for me there is a quandary: people have to learn the art, but I'm not sure they will learn it in a creative writing program.

The creative writing industry produces far more poets than the society can assimilate. It locates writing, and even the consumption of writing, in the university. And that raises enormous problems about the production and reception of literature.

Poets, especially now, are nearly the only people who read poetry, who publish poetry, who go to poetry readings, who write reviews of poetry. It's a closed world in which, little by little, we have been losing the reader as "the other." Now, from some points of view, there's absolutely nothing wrong with a situation where you're overproducing poets and underproducing readers. If you have a sufficient number of writer-readers, maybe it doesn't matter. You have a constituency.

But I believe that there is what I call an incestuous situation, as opposed to a marital situation, and that the situation I just described is an incestuous one. And I have a tendency, as an anthropologist, to believe in the marital system—where the ego, as we say in anthropology, *is concerned with an other,* who is not necessarily a writer. It is the survival of this reader that seems important to me.

Why is it important? Because poetry must communicate. You must have a poetry that stretches out to the whole of society, or to a very significant part of it. In democratic terms, poetry has got to be a big part of *the people,* the American people. If you don't retain that attitude, then you get into a number of extremely solipsistic positions, which is where I think the avant-garde in American poetry is at this moment.

If writers haven't led a life, then there's not much point in writing about it.

Poetry has become so academicized that it needs the academic imprimatur in order to survive. As one publisher put it to me, "Kiddo, if you don't survive with the professors, you're not gonna survive at all."

People will pay me a great deal of money to talk about William Blake or Wordsworth or Whitman or even Plath, but they will not pay me a penny to talk about *me*. Somewhere down the line, if I'm of any interest, somebody will be paid a vast sum to teach me—a vast sum, comparatively, to what a poet could earn out of poetry—but will not be paid a penny to teach herself or himself. And it'll go on down the line. The effect is that our culture has allowed the avant-gardes to be as difficult as they wish to be, not just because they are working, legitimately, against certain boundaries in the art, but for lots of essentially bureaucratic reasons. And that's because the destination is the university, and the destination is highly intellectual. Even the Beats ended up in the academy! Now almost every poet in this country is a teacher!

It's only recently, since the 1960s, with the growth of the conception of anthropology as the daughter of imperialism, that people have realized that the "informant" was an oppressed being who never had a chance to talk for himself or herself except as mediated through anthropological literature. Many anthropologists have written about trying to establish a more dialogic anthropology, in which the informant would come fully into his or her place.

In some curious way, the poet is also oppressed. The poet is oppressed by the canon-making academic, who sits in judgment.

Douglas Unger

Douglas Unger earned his B.A. from the University of Chicago in 1973.

His novels include *Leaving the Land* (Harper & Row, 1984), *El Yanqui* (Harper, 1986), and *The Turkey War* (Harper, 1988). His new novel, *Voices from Silence,* will be published as a Wyatt Book by St. Martin's Press in 1995. He has taught as a member of the English faculty at Syracuse University and elsewhere. He is currently teaching at the University of Nevada, Las Vegas, and is at work on establishing a new international M.F.A. program in creative writing with the department of English.

Unger strikes a stranger as ingenuous, sensitive, and politically concerned. He's plainly sophisticated, yet boyish. He seems to carry a piece of Hyde Park with him: the drive of a rebellious idealist who also has a sense of fun.

DOUGLAS UNGER *Trying to break away*

I don't think there is any one education that a writer needs. Writers simply need to read, and to practice writing, as much as possible. When I was a student in my first year at the University of Chicago, I became obsessed by this idea of how to write, and I found no end of encouragement there to pursue both literary vocations. I also discovered that I wanted to write political novels, and my education there has helped me to do it, partly because of the highly politicized atmosphere of studies when I was an undergraduate.

I view the modern world in terms of large systems of organization, either economic or political, that control circumstances affecting peoples' lives from the outside. These forces seem to me to be much more powerful than individual will, or even the inner resources of individuals. Confronting such forces and fighting against them is heroic in one sense but probably impossible to do successfully. Still, I cast novels in which these large systems are at work on characters' lives. The characters make choices, responding or reacting to circumstances imposed on them by these powerful systems. In my novel *The Turkey War*, it's the capitalist system and the politics of "the good war," the federal bureaucracy of World War II, as seen and felt in an almost Dickensian nightmare from the shop floor of a speeded-up meatpacking industry during that era. In *El Yanqui*, and in the novel I have been working on now for the past five years, *The Disappeared*, it's a despotic military dictatorship soon on its way to becoming a huge and immoral machine of state terrorism. In my first book, *Leaving the Land,* the wholesale reorganization of American farming and agribusiness by means of government policies and an absurdly unstable marketplace are what the characters are up against. All of these forces exist in the real world. I allow them to invade the worlds of my characters, to determine their lives, despite the many other choices they wish to make. Or the choices they *do* make are countered by what happens, so they have to make other choices, often compromises, and they begin to live lives of continuing reactions rather than their natural, human expressions of free will or of fulfilling desires.

This is admittedly pretty close to the traditional "naturalistic" view, both of the world and of literature. I don't necessarily like that idea. In fact, I believe that one disadvantage of mainstream, so-called realistic writing of the past decade, and maybe with the whole mainstream of American realistic fiction, is that it is too fixed as a form, with the naturalist's eye toward social problems, hard times, and hard luck, the down-and-out, the defeated and the humbled. I'd like someday to write differently. But maybe our culture is just saddled with this social need in its fiction, or at least I see it that way. That kind of writing seemed to be everywhere in Chicago when I was a student, and I think it's still there. It was possible to walk around the old stockyards neighborhood and still see and smell the writing of Upton Sinclair, or the Near North Side and tour the streetwise, troubling world of Nelson Algren. It was possible even to imagine I was passing the exact same buildings and bars and insane trading pits that Frank Norris and Theodore Dreiser described. Or to try to follow the crazed flight of Richard Wright's Bigger Thomas on down to the South Side of town, trying to find a place to hide himself. Chicago was and is the kind of city to encourage a realistic, or naturalistic, view of things.

This naturalistic view was also something I came to while watching my father's ranch in South Dakota, and the farms and ranches of his neighbors, begin to go downhill. The story of his ranches is very much in keeping with a kind of inevitable, naturalistic view. We were constantly fleeing progress, industrialization, and macroeconomic forces. My father was a doctor of jurisprudence, practiced law, and taught it; but ranching was what he really wanted to do. While a student at Chicago, and while I was growing up, I spent summers and a good part of the rest of the years working on his ranches. The first one he owned was in Colorado, near Steamboat Springs. A ski resort moved in. Of course, it then became much more profitable to "farm" condominiums in that region than to be a cattle and wheat rancher. So my family moved to a ranch near Craig, Colorado. Then Craig became a boomtown, the natural gas combines moved in, and there was some strange business in that region with changing water rights to funnel them into what became the total fiasco of oil shale exploitation by huge, multinational corporations. The town of Craig went boom and then bust in about ten years. My father fled all that, too, and bought a sheep ranch in South Dakota. While I was working on it, I began to look at the isolated community in that remote part of South Dakota. I saw close up how the failing agricultural economy was affecting the farmers and their families, no matter how efficient they were, no matter how hard they worked, and despite their best efforts to survive. My novel *Leaving the Land* was the direct result of that experience and upbringing.

Before Chicago, I'd spent a significant portion of my time *not* going to school. I led an itinerant life as a teenager. I went to four different schools from junior high to high school, because of split-ups in my family, my parents' divorce, and my own frequent and irresponsible tripping around and just running away. I've lived a lot of lives, and I'm grateful for that. And I keep looking for the *next* life after this one of teaching and writing. I am a writer primarily, and hope to continue to write. But I've lived the life of a rancher, the life of a suburban junior high school student, the life of a wealthy "son" of a privileged family in Argentina. At sixteen, I received an American Field Service scholarship to study for a year in Buenos Aires. Living there, too, was an experience of outside forces affecting one's life. We were under the thumb of a military dictatorship, and increasingly, individual will and choice were subservient to the totalitarian powers of the state. Before and after that, I lived the life of a traveling hippie. I was a draft dodger for a short time, using legal ways to avoid the draft. I've lived the life of a commercial fisherman. Then a journalist. And somewhere in the middle of all that, I lived the life of a U of C student.

At the University of Chicago, I studied very hard, as almost everyone did. When I was lucky enough to get to go to college, I was not looking for the social campus that prevails at many universities; I was looking for an extremely serious place to sit myself down and study. I knew that my education had huge gaps and holes in it. I tremendously admired the university and what it had to offer. I felt privileged and fortunate to be in such a place. I was coming from a very close interaction with the urban environment of Buenos Aires in 1969–70, a highly politicized environment, so, in a way, maybe it was only natural for me to go on to the highly politicized and urban environment of the University of Chicago in 1970.

Those were strange times. The university had just suffered a student strike; the takeover of the administration building had occurred; the antiwar movement was going on. The Weather Underground had only months before vacated their apartments on 57th Street. So the atmosphere was charged. There were important impending things to do in Chicago—studying, certainly, but also politics. Politics *was* an education.

True, the stakes weren't too high at Chicago; it wasn't a matter of life and death to be politically engaged. Or it was so only remotely. It was less personally risky, but still serious business, given the context of the war in Vietnam. In Argentina, it *was* a matter of life and death. Many of the students in my Argentinian school eventually became *Montoneros*—urban guerrillas—beginning with the second administration of Juan Perón, then against the regime of the *comandantes* that followed. As nearly as I can determine, years later, one out of every five students with whom I went to school was either forced into exile or was brutally made to "disappear" because of political activities.

At Chicago, even so, there were many students who treated politics as a matter of life and death. We were working hard toward changing society, or at least we thought we were. We *did* things. We organized antiwar protests; we worked for the Black Panther breakfast program, raising money in Hyde Park to give to storefronts on the South Side, whose goal it was to get school kids who hadn't eaten breakfast a hot meal before school. We also raised money for Jesse Jackson's Operation PUSH activities, or we worked for them and for other community and political causes.

There was an organization called Students for Violent Non-Action that was famous in those days. As far as I know, SVNA was the invention of the student-government president David Affelder and his group of friends. As SVNA leaders, however, they all used the same name, "Frank Malbranche," for the press and other audiences. Affelder and several others had figured out that one of the most important things we could do was to get media attention for the causes in which we believed—rather than taking over an administration building or an ROTC office, getting teargassed, or getting our heads beaten in. For example, we'd set up symbolic barricades on campus for an antiwar protest, modeled, I suppose, after what students were doing in Paris in 1968. Or we'd serve SVNA punch on the main quadrangle. We'd get big cans full of ethanol, which we stole from the chemistry department, and fruit juices and Kool-Aid. We'd set up a vat of highly alcoholic punch on the quad on a good spring day, and there'd be a spontaneous SVNA party at which antiwar and political speeches were given.

We organized a media event down at the Civic Center, a Flush-In for the Environment, with the goal of protesting the amount of raw sewage that was going into the Chicago River and despoiling the lakefront. The "non-action" to be "done" was that at four o'clock on a Friday afternoon, we asked the whole city of Chicago to flush its toilets all at once, claiming that this was certain to cause a tidal wave in Lake Michigan. We advertised this in leaflets and pamphlets, and on radio programs, all over the city. As I recall, the event got TV attention, and the newspapers picked up on it. It was like guerrilla theater.

The Lascivious Arts Ball was invented at that time as a political act. We wanted to treat pornography with humor, to take the notion of sin and exploitation and "lascivious" behavior and turn it into something positive, a huge fund-raising party for the student government association and for SVNA. I was in charge of hiring the striptease dancers. We had both males and females, of course. We invited the pornographic implements dealers and adult bookstore owners in Chicago to set up booths in Ida Noyes Hall and demonstrate their wares. We had a live demonstration of how to make bathtub gin, with a nude model in the bathtub. We had live readings from pornographic novels—I remember giving a reading composed entirely of about five pages of moans, groans, and orgasmic sighing. There was good music, too, and a lot of "clean" lascivious fun.

The university administration was tolerant of our activities, even though we challenged the university and the president, Edward Levi, on many issues. I think they were tolerant because to confront us probably would have drawn yet more attention to us. Also, I think that many professors and administrators were tolerant of us because they basically agreed with what we were doing. And I know that some professors went along with us because they thought we were providing the whole university with some spectacular yet politicized entertainment, and let's face it, the U of C has often needed more of that kind of fun just to relieve the intensity of the pressures.

The sheer quantity of obsessions at the University of Chicago! As a student in the College, you watched thousands of graduate students seriously, crazily, obsessively at work. And some of that rubbed off on you. You got obsessed and crazy. That experience of seriousness was of real value to me. The atmosphere of seriousness about reading, in particular, was of tremendous importance. I probably spend half of my time at the university on the third floor of the Joseph Regenstein Library. That was where I would meet my friends, where I would meet my dates, and where I would sit down with groups on breaks to lay out our various schemes. I would finish up at about 10:30 and go have a quick beer at Jimmy's Woodlawn Tap. And there I'd talk about what I was studying, obsess about it, go to bed late at night, wake up early in the morning, get out to classes, and do more of the same. Reading book after book after book was a very important part of learning to be a writer.

A writer needs to discover a group of writers, or at least one other writer with whom he feels so closely identified that he believes he could have written what the other writer has. Or maybe he feels that he actually *did* write it: "He stole my novel! That's mine! He stole my style!" he thinks. Then he decides, well, he's going to try to do it the same way anyway. The writing he loves and admires really *is* his creation.

Such a moment came for me in Argentina in 1969, when I got my first copy of Gabriel García Márquez's *One Hundred Years of Solitude,* in Spanish, before it had been translated into English. Another such moment for me was hearing Jorge Luis Borges speak in Buenos Aires, listening to that magic and visionary voice. Not that I ever did or even now write remotely like either of these authors—it's the visceral identification with their vocations, with their voices, their styles, that's important. That's the first inspiration to try to write seriously, or at least it was for me. So I owe a debt to Borges, to García Márquez, and to William Faulkner, whose work I discovered because I found out that García Márquez had found in Faulkner his first inspiration. In general, that's the way I first began to read the great writers. When I was in Argentina, I read Edgar Allan Poe for the first time in Spanish. I read Dostoyevsky for the first time in Spanish. I even read Raymond Chandler in Spanish. So I discovered North American and other literatures by an indirect route. Then being a student at the U of C seemed the right place to have had that kind of a crazy education. Without many questions at all, I kept right on with graduate-level classes in Iberian and Latin American literature, so part of my reading was as though I had never changed languages, while at the same time I had the tremendous luxury of beginning to read my own country's writers in the original.

All of my jobs at the university allowed me to read. I had a job with the department of anatomy, under Dr. Ronald Singer and Dr. Robert Oxnard, caretaking animals that were being experimented on. Cleaning their cages and feeding them was something I could get done in an hour, and yet I would have to be there for about four hours. So I'd sit on sacks of monkey feed in the storeroom and read. William S. Burroughs, Eugene Ionesco, Sartre, Thomas Pynchon, John Barth—those are the authors I remember most from that job. That seemed the appropriate place to read them, and the atmosphere really helped to make sense of them. There are passages of Burroughs and Ionesco that I still can't read or listen to without also experiencing the peculiar warm odor of monkey biscuits.

I was also responsible, with some of the permanent staff, for bringing new cadavers to the anatomy lab from time to time. We'd go to a cadaver bank in Chicago and pick them up out of huge tanks filled with formaldehyde, put them in plastic bags, load them in the truck, and drive them back to campus for a very secretive, back-alley delivery. In the lab, each cadaver had a numbered pan. We traded off the job of going up to the lab and collecting in plastic bags each of the body parts the medical students had finished with and left in the pans. We kept track of these in refrigerators downstairs, so that when the whole process was over, it was possible to return the remains to the family and to cremate or bury the body.

This, of course, was one of the most bizarre student jobs on campus at the University of Chicago. In me it inspired a Dostoyevskian phase. The days I worked in the lab, I went home and wrote really turgid, depressing stuff. There was a lot of confronting of mortality and the meaning of life in it—dark, inward, reflective prose, all of it on its way to the wastebasket. At first I was repelled by that job, but it simply paid too well to quit, and there was that precious time to read. Then I experienced an attitude change about the physicality of death, a comfortable sense that the material remains of bodies are something natural, that there's nothing repulsive about them at all; somehow, there was still something very human about them. I learned to feel then and still feel a certain reverence for the humanity of human remains.

After a while I transferred from that job to Chicago Lying-In Hospital as a night admissions clerk, working three or four night shifts a week for about the same pay. Aside from the very occasional emergency, the job just required doing the paperwork for mothers delivering babies, being a small part of that intensely and thoroughly alive and healthy process. The atmosphere was usually pretty happy and joyous, even fun sometimes. Mothers seemed to deliver babies in waves; it was like waiting for the rush at a restaurant. Everyone came in at once, and there were hours of scrambling around, getting the paperwork done, all the doctors and nurses so busy they could barely change gowns and gloves before the next new life came into the world. Then there would usually be a lull for two or three hours before the next rush, and it was possible to sit at the admissions desk and study until then. It was a great job. And a tremendous relief to me to be working so closely with the living.

I brought to the university a pretty sketchy background in Latin American and Spanish literature and a tremendous interest in North American literature. At Chicago, I added German. I did a General Studies in the Humanities B.A. degree which combined Spanish, English, and German literatures, and, in some sense, that's the work I'm still doing, in teaching my own courses, twenty years later— comparative literature, mainly Latin American and North American writers and their influences, or contemporary fiction either in English or in translation, and I'm still learning. Of course, at the U of C I also took courses in classics and in philosophy. I really had the chance to study Spanish literatures with some of the great professors, and I'm still so appreciative of them—the expatriate writer and painter, Francisco Ayala, and George Haley, such a deep and inspiring scholar, who is still teaching there. But Richard Stern, of the English department, the first real writer I ever had the chance to work with, was the one most influential in guiding me into becoming a writer.

Stern was a very good teacher—tough at first, and very rejecting of my work until it *turned,* broke through, became good enough. I made it turn, and he helped me make it turn, by encouraging me to keep doing it—by simply writing a lot, by writing and writing and writing. In fact, I wrote a novel as my bachelor's thesis, some of which was later rewritten and was published as minor parts of *El Yanqui.* I remember that at first I'd hand in turgid, nearly incomprehensible prose, and Stern would look at it and say, kindly enough, but in so many words, "No. I don't like this at all." Then I'd react by writing something even more far out, incomprehensible, experimental, so-called. And he wouldn't like that, either. He was patient. He read everything closely, carefully. I finally just wanted so much to write something he liked. So I pushed through, got honest, and started writing something more real. That was when he let me know that he approved, that writing was what I should be doing, and he really pushed me along.

I also gravitated toward the *Chicago Review*. I became the managing editor, working under editors Alexander Besher, Curt Matthews, and Richard Hack. We handed manuscripts back and forth. We helped to organize readings on campus, and we went up to the Near North Side and the Body Politic Theater and connected with that literary crowd—I remember the poets Ted Berrigan, Bill Knott, Alice Notley, and Tom Lux were all there at that time.

We had fairly radical tastes. Word came to us that William S. Burroughs needed money. The *Chicago Review* had published parts of *Naked Lunch* a decade before. So we approached Kenneth Northcott and the William Vaughn Moody lecture series, and we got Burroughs, Allen Ginsberg, and Lawrence Ferlinghetti to read on campus. Then Burroughs and Ferlinghetti and Ginsberg hung around for a day or two. They stayed in our apartments, and we all lived together like best friends. They were somehow *our* writers then. I've never forgotten how they were much more interested in and paid more attention to us students than to the U of C professors, or to anyone else, and I've tried to be the same way when I'm invited to give readings at colleges and universities.

The *Review* invited Anaïs Nin to give a lecture, and she and I had an argument. I think it was in the car, when I was picking her up from the airport. I'd just read her book on Virginia Woolf, and she was talking about male perspectives on women and female perspectives on men, and seemed to be saying that women can write certain things about women that men can never understand. She was proposing a gender-divided way of reading. And I argued with her, just as a University of Chicago student would, aggressively coming back at her with *on the other hand.* And she grew extremely irritated with me. Of course, her arguments were much sounder than mine. It upset me that I lost the argument, doubly so because she was such a charming and utterly beautiful woman, and I seemed stupidly to have offended her. That overheated discussion stayed with me for years, and now I know it was part of my new obsession to try to write convincingly from a woman's point of view, somehow to show her I was right. Maybe I was wrong then and am dead wrong now, but I still believe that writing and reading are not necessarily gender-divided experiences. I think it's socially damaging to read that way, that when we do we are imposing difficult and erroneous restrictions on the appreciation and understanding of the language, and, worse, we may really only be upholding unjust gender discriminations. In any case, partly as a result of that experience, I finally started writing the first passages of *Leaving the Land* to prove that it is possible for men to write about women in a way that breaks through that kind of gender-based ideology.

Fiction in America was changing. The new avant-garde in the early seventies was really Raymond Carver—a writer very different from the "Beat" or "experimental" or "metafictional" authors who were popular with the so-called counterculture. Back then, Carver had no prominence, was being published only in literary quarterlies, and was going through terrible personal troubles. My first introduction to his writing was a story, "They're Not Your Husband," that came to the *Chicago Review* office hand-carried by Richard Hack. The story had been passed on to him, in manuscript, by Curt Johnson, of December Press. Hack brought it in and said we all had to read that story right away. And it really was something new, a kind of writing that seemed to bring us all back to reality. When we published that story, little did I know that a few years later, not only would I meet Raymond Carver, but I would become a part of his family. I had no idea of that then, but I began to read all his work that I could find, and it changed the way I looked at my own writing.

Still, the *Chicago Review* at that time adhered to a philosophy of publishing mainly experimental literature. But I began to wonder what was really experimental and what wasn't, and I became very unsure, thinking that maybe the new realistic stories we were sometimes publishing, like Carver's, or one of the "Murphy" stories by Mark Costello, and other stories, might be the real innovations in those days. Our culture, though, currently suffers from an almost total commitment to realism. I now wish there were room for much more postmodern and surrealist work, not necessarily the overkilled so-called experimental stories of that era but something truly new and innovative. I guess I'm starting to look for more of that kind of writing now. My own writing has a foothold in realism; I resist total fantasy, and attempts at surrealism almost always seem forced and false. And yet I feel shackled by realism, frustrated that, stylistically, there's so little diversity. I wish I could break away from realism successfully. That's something that hasn't changed. As a student writer, I was also trying to break away.

During my time with the *Chicago Review,* our problems were with reorganization more than anything else. We thought we were trying to establish more independence from the university, but what was really going on was that the university had almost completely lost interest in us. The *Review* goes through eras, and when the new group of editors, headed by Alexander Besher and Curt Matthews— the people who later created Chicago Review Press—took over, the magazine was in one of its down periods. Its subscription list was a mess, and the magazine was close to totally broke, in danger of shutting down. Somehow, we managed to scrounge around for unused funds at various university departments and get them. And Herman Sinaiko helped with the reading series, with a fund he controlled, and that was a huge help in keeping things going. Somehow, as I guess always has happened, enough concerned U of C people stepped in and gave new energy to the magazine and kept it alive. Then the Playboy Foundation, located just downtown, gave us $16,000. It was quite an evening when the editors of the *Review* were invited to the Playboy Mansion for the ceremony, and we watched our check being served up on a tray by a Playboy bunny. The staff—men and women—had the run of the club after the ceremony, and couldn't have had a better time.

The feeling of being a part of the life of the mind and of the great tradition at Chicago was certainly nurturing to me, but as a student approaching a course of study, I think I had less management—less direction—than I would have found at a lot of other universities. I was on my own a lot. Of course, never entirely alone—Richard Stern and William Veeder were there for my writing, and Francisco Ayala and George Haley were there for me in other ways. I always had someone who gave me real criticism—not soft, too nice, but real, honest readings and reactions. Still, there were times when I had no idea what I was doing or why, sort of let loose to make up my own curriculum as I went along. I'm very glad of that experience now. Being a student at the University of Chicago prepared me well for the life of a writer.

I also believe very much in teaching. When I go into a classroom now, as a professor, I have in mind certain of my Chicago professors and the way they taught. I find myself imitating the gestures of those professors, and even the intonations of their voices. Sometimes, after teaching a class, when I've been a kind of living echo of a teacher I studied with and recognize that with a kind of amazement similar to a déjà vu, I sit and wonder if maybe they were doing the same to me in the classroom, so that in a multigenerational, ancestral way, not only has knowledge descended, and the conscious forms of teaching, but many of the actual voices and gestures, too, the whole *physicality* of teaching, that subconscious and active part of it, has been passed on. There's a kind of pleasant spookiness in this feeling, and I wonder if the whole subconscious nature of any teacher's actions in a classroom, descending for uncountable generations, may actually be just as important as—even more important than—any abstract knowledge that's being taught. I'm probably wrong. But I think many teachers feel this way at times.

There are a lot of people in my mind, from the U of C, when I'm teaching. I think a great deal about Herman Sinaiko, the way he paced the room, how he could fill almost every inch of a chalkboard with scatterings of ideas and notes, and how he was constantly running his hands through his hair and teaching *at* us, using the Socratic method in a way that permitted and acknowledged and honored a question, but also let us know what his answer to it was, physically, before he'd even said a word, and then how he would make us go after that answer until we came up with it ourselves. George Haley is also in my mind a great deal for the scholarly demands he made, in such a pleasant and seemingly undemanding way, and for teaching what it is to research an idea in literature, what it is to follow the pathways of a bibliography, to know what you're writing about before you write it, and to be a taskmaster about the logic of an essay. When I'm writing fiction and teaching writing workshops, one of the good voices in my head is Richard Stern's. I'll pause and wonder, "Hmmm. How would he take this? What would he say in this situation?" And there's an invaluable way I learned from him of praising or withholding praise from eager young writers that seems to work, at least for some, to change their writing.

Yet even after saying all of this, the disciplines of scholarship and of literary studies don't, I think, directly affect what I decide to write or the way I write when I'm working on creating a fiction. I don't think that writing fiction is something that's done in the head first and then translated to the page. For me, fiction is something that comes from somewhere else, another center of one's being—and that's what comes out first. Sometimes it comes out in a disorganized way; often, for me, it comes out in an overwritten way. The problem then is to use one's knowledge of literature, the disciplines of scholarship and literary studies, one's capacities as a critic and an editor, to look back over all that raw material and begin all the reshaping and rewriting that, for me at least, can go on for years.

Certainly political and social ideas, which are intellectual, come out in my work. I've succeeded and failed in handling them at various times. But I'm still trying to do it, find the right balance, even to break away—and do it *right*.

Kurt Vonnegut

Kurt Vonnegut attended the University of Chicago as a World War II veteran from 1945 to 1947. His Chicago M.A. in anthropology was awarded on the basis of his novel *Cat's Cradle* (Holt, 1963) in 1971.

Vonnegut's many books include *Player Piano* (Scribner's, 1952), *Mother Night* (Fawcett, 1962), *God Bless You, Mr. Rosewater* (Holt, 1965), *Welcome to the Monkey House* (Dell, 1970), *Happy Birthday, Wanda June* (Dell, 1971), *Breakfast of Champions* (Seymour Lawrence/Delacorte, 1973), *Slaughterhouse-Five* (Seymour Lawrence/Delacorte, 1973), *Fates Worse than Death* (Putnam, 1991), and *Wampeters, Foma, and Granfalloons* (Dell, 1992).

When Vonnegut sat down to talk about Chicago in his Manhattan town house, his conversation was filled with wry, waggish, or indignant interjections about injustices past and present, personal, social, and larger. His affability was unmuffled, and yet he always had—and used—a critical edge.

KURT VONNEGUT *A very*
fringe character

I thought a hell of a lot of the University of Chicago, and Chicago didn't think a damn thing about me. I was a very fringe character in the anthropology department.

Before Chicago, I had never been a liberal arts or social science major; I'd had chemistry at Cornell. And after Cornell, I was three years in the goddamned infantry in World War II. That tore a big chunk out of my life.

The University of Chicago gave returning veterans a test on what they knew generally. They took my credits, which were in physics, chemistry, and math, and admitted me as a graduate student in anthropology.

After going through the war and all, I thought man was the thing to study. I really think it ought to be done in second grade, but better in graduate school than nowhere else. And it *was* interesting.

I had about three years of credits from Cornell, so I was one year short of a bachelor's. But in the Hutchins system, a bachelor's degree was given after two years, and I couldn't get one.

And so, I had at least three years to go for a master's. That was okay with me, because it was a very exciting time in my life.

I was ready. I was like Thomas Wolfe when he went to college, so excited that he was running through the woods and jumping over stone walls and barking like a dog.

Hell, I'd been an army private—I'd had a lousy life for three years. So the university was sheer luxury. The intellectual kick was great.

But I had a wife and kids, and I wrote a thesis which was rejected by the U of C.

When I wasn't in class, I was working as a reporter at the Chicago City News Bureau. I also spent a lot of time with my family, rather than at the university. I led a pretty separate life, because I had a wife and kids. Most students didn't. And in the summers, other people would go off on digs or do fieldwork, but I couldn't. Because I had a wife and kids, I had to keep working.

We had one superstar in the anthropology department, Robert Redfield. Victorian anthropology had been completely discredited, because cultural as well as physical evolution was assumed by the Victorians: they believed that people progressed from polygamy to monogamy, from many gods to one, and so on. Redfield said, "Now, wait a minute: there is one stage that every society goes through, and I'll describe it." He called it the folk society.

The folk society was closed, isolated from outsiders. It included a common belief system and extensive kinship relationships. It sounds very comfortable, like what everybody's looking for.

I looked on the University of Chicago community as a folk society—and I felt like an outsider in it. I felt excluded by that bunch in the department, although they had admitted me. I wasn't treated badly, but they already *had* a family.

My ironic distance as a novelist has a lot to do with having been an anthropology student. Anthropology made me a cultural relativist, which is what everybody ought to be. People the world over ought to be taught, seriously, that culture is a gadget, and that one culture is as arbitrary as another.

That's an important lesson, yet some people never hear of it. Then, when they're adult, they can't *bear* to hear of it.

Culture *is* a gadget; it's something we inherit. And you

can fix it the way you can fix a broken oil burner. You can fix it constitutionally.

In my master's thesis, I studied what it takes to effect radical cultural change. What kind of a group do you need to put society through a 45-degree turn, or a 90-degree turn? It appeared that what you needed was an authentic genius. Really, you need two very bright guys who have status in the community. One of them says, about the genius, "This guy is *not* nuts." And then, you also need an explainer. For the Cubists, there was Picasso, and there were Braque and Apollinaire, who explained what they were doing. (Picasso wasn't about to explain what the hell he was doing. That would have been too tiresome.)

My thesis considered the Cubists and the Native American ghost dance. An intensely bright professor named Sidney Slotkin worked with me on it. Slotkin, too, was marginal in the anthropology department, although he had come out of it; he just wasn't their kind.

I studied how change can be made—but a novelist can't make change. You can't. There's no willpower. How dare somebody who is not a journalist or does not hold rank of some kind comment on something as complicated as military logistics or foreign policy or petroleum? Who the hell are you? And you're gonna say what the government should do next?

The novelist is in a funny position: utterly unqualified. Having no badge or rank, and cracking off about this or that. It peeves a lot of people. How dare we do what we do?

Yet novelists can have a great effect on young people. When I was between the ages of fourteen and twenty and starting to read just about anything, I had no immunity whatsoever to ideas. I would read Hemingway, Steinbeck, Dos Passos, and James T. Farrell—and their political opinions would become mine.

I assume that some kids have become pacifists because

of me. Actually, I'm not even sure what my message as a novelist is. But I would like to infect people with humane ideas before they're able to defend themselves.

My boyhood dream was to cure cancer. Not much chance of that. My brother was a scientist, so I was going to be a scientist.

There were all these things I wanted to be, instead of what I am.

My father had talked for a long time about my becoming an architect, but then he became filled with self-pity and said, "Be anything but an architect."

If everything had gone right, right now I would be an architect in Indianapolis. But instead I went to Cornell to be a chemist.

And if everything had gone right in Chicago, I would be a newspaper reporter or a managing editor—or busting a strike!

The Chicago City News Bureau, where I worked when I was in graduate school, was a cocky operation. We were outlaws. It's where a lot of journalists in Chicago start. The theory was that working for City News was the only way you'd be able to get a job on a Chicago newspaper. You *had* to start there.

I could do at City News what I can't do now, which is walk into any part of town anywhere and start talking to people about their lives.

As a reporter, I'd go to police station after police station after police station, call on firehouses, and then I'd go and call the coast guard: "Anything going on?" For eight hours I'd be on the South Side, the North Side, the West Side.

We were all looking around for everything. Some of the reporters carried guns.

One time I found a body.

I had started out as a copyboy, just stuck there in the office, waiting for somebody to move on so I could become a reporter. One Sunday I was there and had the police radio on. I heard that in an office building three blocks over, a guy had just been killed in an elevator accident. There was nobody else to go, so I went over, and I got there as soon as the fire department and police did.

The top of the elevator had come down and crushed the elevator operator. And so I got to see this guy squashed and dead.

I phoned the story in, and my editor said, "Okay, call up his wife. What does his wife say?"

I said, "I can't do that."

He said, "Yes, you can."

Oh, it was so dishonorable! I wouldn't do it now. If I had worked at City News much longer, I probably would have gotten sick of it.

Still, being a journalist influenced me as a novelist. I mean, a lot of critics think I'm stupid because my sentences are so simple and my method is so direct: they think these are defects. No. The point is to write as much as you know as quickly as possible.

In journalism you learn to write a story so someone can cut it without even reading it, putting all the most important stuff in the beginning. And in my books, for the first few pages I say what the hell is going to happen. When I taught at the University of Iowa Writers Workshop, I told my students, "Look, I want you to write in such a way that should you drop dead, the reader ought to be able to finish the story for you."

I wasn't writing fiction in Chicago, just news and anthropology papers. Later, I started writing short stories and selling them. So I said, Hey, I'm a writer, I guess!

When I left the university, there was a list of jobs open for anthropologists tacked on the department bulletin board. All of those jobs were for Ph.D.'s, of course.

I got offered a job in public relations by General Elec-

Kurt Vonnegut   240

tric and figured I'd better take it. I had a wife and kids, and just couldn't hold on any longer. So they hired me.

Particularly if you were a child of the Depression, in those days you just got a job. And you didn't feel destined for this or that job—you just got any goddamned job.

Later on, I was living on Cape Cod and needed to make a living. I wanted to teach high school, but I had no college degree. Since Chicago had turned down my thesis, I had about seven years of college and no degree.

So I wrote the people at Chicago a letter saying, "Hey, look, you guys, I'm way past a bachelor's. Won't you at least give me a bachelor's degree?"

And they said, "No. We're sorry, but you would have to come back here and take a course." It was Survey of Civilization, or something. There was no chance of my doing that; by then I had six kids.

So there I was, without any degree. Otherwise I would have become a teacher. I was quite angry about it.

I wrote *another* thesis, about the mathematical shapes of stories. That one was rejected, too.

It got worse. Finally I was on the faculty at Harvard, without a degree, and I had stopped bothering Chicago. I received a letter from a guy at Chicago who had taken over the division of social sciences.

He wrote, "I have just become dean of social sciences here, I was looking through a file, and I found an enormous envelope with your name on it. So I read it." And he added, "I am pleased to tell you that under the rules of the university, you have always been entitled to a master's degree, for having published a book of quality."

Cat's Cradle is what qualified me for a master's degree.

That novel was anthropology, but *invented* anthropology: in it, I wrote about an invented society.

So I had been entitled to an M.A. all along.

When my father was dying, he said, "I want to thank you, because you've never put a villain in any of your stories." The secret ingredient in my books is, there has never been a villain.

Some of the cultures we studied at Chicago were quite gruesome. The Aztecs were really scary, cutting people's hearts out. The Mayans weren't much better. And there have been instances of terrible cruelty even in benign societies, living in peace.

Society can be a villain, just the way a mother can be.

Yet it seems to me that it's no more trouble to be virtuous than to be vicious. I'm critical, but not a pessimist.

Look at all that humans can do! They're versatile. They can ride a unicycle. They can play the harp. They can, apparently, do *anything*.

Anyway, I liked the University of Chicago. They didn't like *me*.

Marguerite Young

Marguerite Young earned an M.A. from the University of Chicago in 1936, and went on to teach at the University of Iowa, Columbia University, and for many years at the New School for Social Research in New York City.

Her books include the novel *Miss MacIntosh, My Darling* (Scribner's, 1965, Dalkey Archive, 1993), eighteen years in the writing, and *Prismatic Ground* (Macmillan, 1937), *Moderate Fable* (Reynal & Hitchcock, 1945), *Angel in the Forest* (Scribner's, 1966), *The Collected Poems of Marguerite Young* (Arundel, 1990), and *Nothing but the Truth* (Carlton, 1992).

Part of the inspiration for *Miss MacIntosh* came from Young's time in Hyde Park. Talking at length in a New York City coffee shop, Young recalled the experiences of her student self with operatic richness and flourish, as if real life were the best fantasy.

MARGUERITE YOUNG *A vacation from the modern world*

As I've always said, I don't know where I got my education—at the University of Chicago or at the opium lady's.

Oh, some of the weirdest, wildest, most marvelous characters I met in that place! Including the man who tried to assassinate the Czar of Russia. And then, the Czarina was supposedly a university student. I heard she was a mental case, brought there by a guardian from West Chicago. She thought she was Anastasia Romanov.

The most amazing and enlightening years of my life were spent at the university.

My life is centered completely on Chicago; here in New York, I'm just an exile. And that's true of many Midwesterners. I think of going back; I think of going back and living in Chicago.

Everything that I was ever to be or become was in those Chicago years.

I was born in Indianapolis. Many of us had never been more than twenty miles from home. And so a group of us, young writers from Indianapolis, decided to go to Chicago, just to see the city. We had never been there.

I had graduated from Butler University, a small Christian college in Indianapolis, and had no money. This was in the heart of the Depression, when no one could afford to go to graduate school. Furthermore, women were not particularly welcome.

While we were in Chicago, I was supposed to meet a friend down at the university's Rockefeller Chapel. And

Lionel said, "If I'm not there, give me another hour, walk around, and come back." Then we would all go home.

So I arrived, and he wasn't there. I strolled around, and happened to pass by the admissions office.

Well, I thought, I'll just go in and apply for entrance into the University of Chicago.

I had a net worth, at that time, of eighty dollars—and absolutely nothing else. And no reason to think that I would ever be accepted by the university. Anyhow, I went in and applied for admission out of curiosity.

A young man looked at my application and asked, "Are you going to be on the campus long?"

"For about an hour."

He said, "Well, take a walk around." It was 11:30. "Be here at 12:30, and I'll speak to you again about your application."

So I walked around, came back. He said, "I have called the various deans and department heads. The University of Chicago wishes to offer you a fellowship. Your fellowship will begin in exactly two weeks. Come to the University of Chicago!"

In exactly two weeks I came back and enrolled to get my master's degree at the university.

It was a great university. It was an elitist school with a vengeance, and I think a school should be elitist. Chicago took the most aristocratic approach to literature, to the humanities, philosophy, art, everything. The highest intellectual and artistic standards were imposed.

I studied with Ronald Salmon Crane, whom I adored, and with Robert Morss Lovett. I studied with T. V. Smith, a wonderful professor of philosophy. I studied with H. Baskerville, the Elizabethan fairy-tale man. He knew more about fairies than anyone in the world at the time.

Ronald Crane's favorite student was Elder Olson. I got

my desk at the library positioned in such a way that I could look straight at Elder Olson. Only he didn't know *me*.

In Crane's class, we read *Tom Jones* thirteen times. I said the mistake was the fourteenth. Crane was a great institution. But oh, he was so haughty! And so distant from his students.

When my book *Angel in the Forest* came out, I received a telegram from him. "Is it possible that you are the same Marguerite Young who was in my class at the University of Chicago? If so, let me tell you of the great pride I feel in your work." And I wired back, "It is indeed possible. It's absolutely true that I was in your class. And to have known you was one of the great experiences of my life." Which it was. You cannot fool me as to aesthetics or criticism.

At the other extreme was Robert Morss Lovett, who lived at Hull House and was a revolutionary. He taught Milton, Dante, Cromwell, the fall of man. He was a radical, and he taught as if everything had happened in Chicago yesterday.

Lovett would say to us, "For the benefit of any Hearst spies who may be secreted in this classroom, Oliver Cromwell lived in the seventeenth century." He taught the literature of revolution and utopia, and philosophy, and history, the consciousness of history.

When I was a student at the university, I felt it was my responsibility to know and read *everything*. How to get away from just aping your contemporaries was the thing.

Who was the most remarkable person I've ever known in my life? It was Minna K. Weissenbach, the opium lady in Hyde Park.

Although as a student I had received a fellowship, I had no money apart from that. So I had to earn about one hundred dollars a quarter, and I got a job—various jobs.

Eventually I grew anxious to get a better job than the one I had. I was working as a receptionist at the Eleanor Club, where out-of-town students lived, and the job was almost killing me with long hours. Some students stayed out all night, and I was the one who had to let them in.

So I applied for a job at the employment office of the university. They knew of a woman, Minna K. Weissenbach, who was looking for a secretary. I called her three times and got no answer. Called a fourth time and said, "I am a University of Chicago student working on my master's degree."

Said she, "I'm looking for someone to take a vacation with me away from the modern world. Would you like to come?"

"*Yes.*"

This woman wanted me to read Shakespeare to her. She paid me for reading Shakespeare aloud.

She was an opium eater. "If I am passing into an opium dream," she told me, "pay no attention. Just go ahead and read—or go home."

Whether or not she actually heard the Shakespeare hardly mattered.

Everyone fell under the spell of the opium lady.

I would stay all night at her house and sleep. She would say, "You can sleep in Millay's bed." Oh, my God! I could have died of ecstasy at the very thought. The opium lady was one of Edna St. Vincent Millay's first patrons at the university; Millay had stayed with her on occasion.

She also said she had a mad brother who was Roosevelt's adviser on the New Deal but who might get out of the asylum at any minute and come and kill everybody.

How would that affect me? Would I be afraid to continue working for her?

I said no, it wouldn't matter.

I saw the opium lady three times a week. She often passed into a coma while I was with her and would speak her dreams aloud. Her hallucinations were the most extraordinary conversations that anyone could wish to hear.

I had been working with her in her house on Drexel Avenue for some time before I began to notice exactly where

I was. And all I saw! Her Bible, in silver covers embossed with gold, jade, onyx. A lamp by her bed called Mr. Res Tacamah after a man in her dreams. (I included the lamp in my novel, *Miss MacIntosh, My Darling*.) The opium lady also had fabulous drinking glasses designed by Mozart. You could play them with a spoon; they made music. She had a medieval table whose chairs were supposed to represent kings and queens out of the Canterbury pilgrimage.

Our friendship became intimate. We would talk from lunch until midnight and through to breakfast the next morning. Some of the time, I would be there in the company of Thornton Wilder or I. B. Libson, a Chicago attorney who came every night to woo the opium lady.

He was sensible. She was not. Oh, it was complicated.

In my writing, the unconscious is very important. And certainly, you couldn't live in the opium lady's house and think the rational *was* important. Instead, it was the surreal, the dream.

At Chicago, with my roommate Jean Garrigue, I wrote poetry day and night. We lived in a studio apartment in Hyde Park.

It was at Chicago, too, that I met Gertrude Stein, Alice B. Toklas, and Thornton Wilder.

I first met Thornton at the opium lady's house; he was there with Gertrude Stein because he was playing host to her during her visit to the university.

Gertrude surprised me. Her hair was close cropped, and she wore a beautiful robe with gold and silver stitches. And she had a dog named Basket, whom she carried with her. She also carried a shepherd's staff, wore sandals, and wore a basket hat. We were told that Spanish peasants had thought she was a wandering friar and made the sign of the cross when they saw her coming.

In Chicago, people just about did that.

Thornton allowed Gertrude to be interviewed by students but wouldn't let them interview Alice B. Toklas, because she was a lesbian; that's what we heard. It was feared that we might get an idea of what lesbians were. I remember Jean Garrigue and I and about nine others peeked out into the hallway and saw Alice there, looking stooped and haggard like an old witch. And we said to each other, "Well, *that's* what lesbians look like!" and then, "Oh, poor Gertrude. She has to live with *her?*" We somehow thought that Alice B. Toklas had Gertrude under *her* spell and that Gertrude was innocent.

There never were such dumbbells. We were absolutely stupid.

At about the same time, I also met Harriet Monroe, the editor of *Poetry*. She was wonderful to me. Kept telling me, "It's all right to be unmarried and literary when you're young; you're so busy with your writing that you don't want to get married. But when you're older, it's lonesome." She was unmarried. The windowsills of her apartment were lined with dolls and Chinese lanterns.

I heard from her the day before she died. She was climbing the mountains in Peru, and wrote, "I don't know why it is. We're here high up in the Andes as we climb along, and I think of you. I see the faces of these people who have subsisted on less than nothing, and there is hardly air to breathe, and I think of you as an example of courage in that way." And the next day she died.

Though not while I was at Chicago, I also knew Kurt Vonnegut—another Chicago student at a different time. In Indiana, I was an assistant homeroom teacher for a while, and in that homeroom was Kurt, one of my students. He had a glass in which he kept live grasshoppers. The glass had holes in it so they could breathe; then he would put his hand over it and watch them die. He was experimenting— what would happen if . . . ? He was writing science fiction, of a kind. He was a rebel, and brilliant. I'm very fond of him. He's a man of good nature.

When I was an undergraduate at Butler University, I had wanted to be a criminologist. I also wanted to be secretary to the printers union. I wanted to work for John L. Lewis. Can you imagine that? I was a junior in college, and they all said, "Oh, Marguerite! You're too sensitive. You're a poet. You would be depressed if you became a social worker. You stick to poetry." So I did.

The first poem I ever wrote was about utopia. I was seven years old and recited the poem to my grandmother, who wrote it down.

At seven I had already lost my father and my mother. They had both married again, but had not taken me or my sister with them. We were abandoned children; all that was meaningful in life had been lost.

I was living with my grandmother. She was an angelic, brilliant woman; whatever I am, I owe to her. She exalted me as *the* writer.

As a child, I would be writing books, and my grandmother would go to the door to answer a caller, and she'd say, "You can't come into the parlor. My granddaughter is writing; she can't be disturbed." I had my manuscripts spread all over the floor, just as I do now, by the way. "Come to the side door, and I'll let you in. My granddaughter is a writer, you know."

My grandmother said to me, "When God created the world, he gave many gifts to many people. He did *not* give you great wealth; he did not give you this, that, and the other. Your parents were even taken away from you. But He did give you one thing. The day you were created, He took out His rarest bolt of silks and satins, embroidered with beasts and birds and flowers, the beautiful things of the universe, and he cut a piece off that bolt and gave it to you. You are a favorite of God. You were born with genius."

I was brought up to believe in writing as the most important thing in life.

Other Chicago Writers

This supplementary list compiled with the help of several advisers, includes some of the fiction writers, poets, translators, journalists, critics, and a few editors who have been associated, at one time or another, in one way or another, with the University of Chicago. The list is supplementary in the sense that writers interviewed for this book are not included.

Jonathan Aaron	Peter Cooley	Thomas Glynn
Ellen Akins	Stanley Crawford	Albert Goldman
Robert Anderson	J. V. Cunningham	Paul Goodman
Ivan Arguelles	Shouri Daniels	Andrew Greeley
Jose Arguelles	Michael Denneny	Emily Grosholz
Aaron Asher	Reuel Denney	John Gunther
Sally Banes	Edwin Diamond	William Harmon
Marvin Bell	George Dillon	Robert Herrick
Randy Blasing	Michael Donaghy	Seymour Hersh
Allan Bloom	Mircea Eliade	Daryl Hine
David Blum	Joseph Epstein	Bette Howland
Wayne Booth	Harold Evans	William Hunt
Marie Boroff	Ronald Fair	Judson Jerome
Carol Brightman	Lauren Fairbanks	H. J. Kaplan
June Rachuy Brindel	James T. Farrell	David Kehr
David Broder	Vardis Fisher	Galway Kinnell
David Brooks	Robert Flanagan	Chidi Ukangwa Ebee Ikonne
William Carpenter	Janet Flanner ("Genet")	Peter LaSalle
Selma Jeanne Cohen	Dorothy Foltz	Naomi Lazard
Michael Collins	Jean Garrigue	William Lehr

James Weber Linn

Meyer Levin

Steve Levine

Robert Morss Lovett

Mina Loy

Norman Maclean

Jackson Mac Low

Tom Mandel

S. J. Marks

Dexter Masters

Campbell McGrath

Peter Michelson

Willard Motley

C. M. Naim

John Frederick Nims

David Oates

Frank O'Hara

Elder Olson

Sara Paretsky

A. B. Paulson

John Podhoretz

Bernard Pomerance

Melinda Popham

Robert Pirsig

James Purdy

Henry Rago

Carl Rakosi

A. K. Ramanujan

David Ray

James Reiss

Elizabeth Madox Roberts

Edouard Roditi

Thomas Rogers

Alane Rollings

Harold Rosenberg

Isaac Rosenfeld

Leo Rosten

Carl Sagan

Aram Saroyan

James Schiffer

Cathleen Schine

Dennis Schmitz

Sarah Schulman

Richard Sennett

Vincent Sheean

Robert Silvers

Ted Solotaroff

Sharon Solwitz

Radcliffe Squires

Brent Staples

Stephen Stepanchev

John Taggart

Mike Taibi

Barry Targan

Studs Terkel

Constantine Trypanis

Jonathan Valin

Carl Van Vechten

Nicholas von Hoffman

Leslie Waller

Lucy Wang

Glenway Wescott

Thornton Wilder

Eugene Wildman

Lanford Wilson

Yvor Winters

Austin Wright

INDEX

Strauss, Leo, 165, 167, 185
Streeter, Robert, 89

Tarcov, Oscar, 3, 5
Tardits, Claude, 204
Tarn, Nathaniel, 199–215
Tate, Allen, 28, 100, 183, 187, 188
Tave, Stuart, 79–80, 83–84, 173
Tax, Sol, 206
Toklas, Alice B., 248–49
Tugwell, Rexford, 31
Turner, Victor, 7, 8

Unger, Douglas, 217–33

Veeder, William, 231
Vonnegut, Kurt, 235–42, 249

Wasiolek, Edward, 135, 141
Wasserman, Jacob, 6
Weissenbach, Minna K., 244, 246–48
Wescott, Glenway, 94, 98
Wilder, Thornton, 120–21, 248–49
Williams, Ellen Bremner, 140
Williamson, George, 32
Wilt, Napier, 17–20, 32, 125
Winters, Yvor, 36, 94–96, 98, 99
Wirth, Louis, 2–3
Wright, Richard, 219

Young, Marguerite, 243–50

Zabel, Morton Dauwen, 125, 173, 176